PROGRAMMER'S
Q U I C K
REFERE
S E R

MS-DOS®
FUNCTIONS

□ □ □ □ □

R A Y   D U N C A N

Microsoft
P R E S S
®

PUBLISHED BY
Microsoft Press
A Division of Microsoft Corporation
16011 NE 36th Way, Box 97017, Redmond, Washington 98073-9717

Library of Congress Cataloging in Publication Data

Duncan, Ray, 1952-
MS-DOS functions.
1. MS-DOS (Computer operating system)   I. Title.
QA76.76.063D859   1988   005.4'46   88-5161
ISBN 1-55615-128-4

Printed and bound in the United States of America.

1 2 3 4 5 6 7 8 9   WAKWAK   3 2 1 0 9 8

Distributed to the book trade in the United States
by Harper & Row.

Distributed to the book trade in Canada by General
Publishing Company, Ltd.

Distributed to the book trade outside the United States
and Canada by Penguin Books Ltd.

Penguin Books Ltd., Harmondsworth, Middlesex, England
Penguin Books Australia Ltd., Ringwood, Victoria, Australia
Penguin Books N.Z. Ltd., 182-190 Wairau Road, Auckland 10,
New Zealand

British Cataloging in Publication Data available

Int 21H Function Summary by Category

Hex	Dec	Function Name	Vers	F/H
Character I/O				
01H	1	Character Input with Echo	1.0+	
02H	2	Character Output	1.0+	
03H	3	Auxiliary Input	1.0+	
04H	4	Auxiliary Output	1.0+	
05H	5	Printer Output	1.0+	
06H	6	Direct Console I/O	1.0+	
07H	7	Unfiltered Character Input Without Echo	1.0+	
08H	8	Character Input Without Echo	1.0+	
09H	9	Display String	1.0+	
0AH	10	Buffered Keyboard Input	1.0+	
0BH	11	Check Input Status	1.0+	
0CH	12	Flush Input Buffer and Then Input	1.0+	
File Operations				
0FH	15	Open File	1.0+	F
10H	16	Close File	1.0+	F
11H	17	Find First File	1.0+	F
12H	18	Find Next File	1.0+	F
13H	19	Delete File	1.0+	F
16H	22	Create File	1.0+	F
17H	23	Rename File	1.0+	F
23H	35	Get File Size	1.0+	F
29H	41	Parse Filename	1.0+	F
3CH	60	Create File	2.0+	H
3DH	61	Open File	2.0+	H
3EH	62	Close File	2.0+	H
41H	65	Delete File	2.0+	H
43H	67	Get or Set File Attributes	2.0+	
45H	69	Duplicate Handle	2.0+	
46H	70	Redirect Handle	2.0+	
4EH	78	Find First File	2.0+	H
4FH	79	Find Next File	2.0+	H

(continued)

Hex	Dec	Function Name	Vers	F/H
File Operations *(cont.)*				
56H	86	Rename File	2.0+	
57H	87	Get or Set File Date and Time	2.0+	H
5AH	90	Create Temporary File	3.0+	H
5BH	91	Create New File	3.0+	H
67H	103	Set Handle Count	3.3+	
68H	104	Commit File	3.3+	H
Record Operations				
14H	20	Sequential Read	1.0+	F
15H	21	Sequential Write	1.0+	F
1AH	26	Set DTA Address	1.0+	
21H	33	Random Read	1.0+	F
22H	34	Random Write	1.0+	F
24H	36	Set Relative Record Number	1.0+	F
27H	39	Random Block Read	1.0+	F
28H	40	Random Block Write	1.0+	F
2FH	47	Get DTA Address	2.0+	
3FH	63	Read File or Device	2.0+	H
40H	64	Write File or Device	2.0+	H
42H	66	Set File Pointer	2.0+	H
5CH	92	Lock or Unlock File Region	3.0+	H
Directory Operations				
39H	57	Create Directory	2.0+	
3AH	58	Delete Directory	2.0+	
3BH	59	Set Current Directory	2.0+	
47H	71	Get Current Directory	2.0+	
Disk Management				
0DH	13	Disk Reset	1.0+	
0EH	14	Select Disk	1.0+	
19H	25	Get Current Disk	1.0+	
1BH	27	Get Default Drive Data	1.0+	
1CH	28	Get Drive Data	2.0+	
2EH	46	Set Verify Flag	1.0+	
36H	54	Get Drive Allocation Information	2.0+	
54H	84	Get Verify Flag	2.0+	

(continued)

2

Hex	Dec	Function Name	Vers	F/H

Process Management

Hex	Dec	Function Name	Vers
00H	0	Terminate Process	1.0+
26H	38	Create New PSP	1.0+
31H	49	Terminate and Stay Resident	2.0+
4BH	75	Execute Program (EXEC)	2.0+
4CH	76	Terminate Process with Return Code	2.0+
4DH	77	Get Return Code	2.0+
62H	98	Get PSP Address	3.0+

Memory Management

Hex	Dec	Function Name	Vers
48H	72	Allocate Memory Block	2.0+
49H	73	Release Memory Block	2.0+
4AH	74	Resize Memory Block	2.0+
58H	88	Get or Set Allocation Strategy	3.0+
5EH	94	Get Machine Name, Get or Set Printer Setup	3.1+
5FH	95	Device Redirection	3.1+

Time and Date

Hex	Dec	Function Name	Vers
2AH	42	Get Date	1.0+
2BH	43	Set Date	1.0+
2CH	44	Get Time	1.0+
2DH	45	Set Time	1.0+

Miscellaneous System Functions

Hex	Dec	Function Name	Vers
25H	37	Set Interrupt Vector	1.0+
30H	48	Get MS-DOS Version Number	2.0+
33H	51	Get or Set Break Flag	2.0+
35H	53	Get Interrupt Vector	2.0+
38H	56	Get or Set Country Information	2.0+
44H	68	IOCTL (I/O Control)	2.0+
59H	89	Get Extended Error Information	3.0+
63H	99	Get Lead Byte Table	2.25 only
65H	101	Get Extended Country Information	3.3+
66H	102	Get or Set Code Page	3.3+

(continued)

Hex	Dec	Function Name	Hex	Dec	Function Name
Reserved Functions			**Reserved Functions** *(cont.)*		
18H	24	Reserved	51H	81	Reserved
1DH	29	Reserved	52H	82	Reserved
1EH	30	Reserved	53H	83	Reserved
1FH	31	Reserved	55H	85	Reserved
20H	32	Reserved	5DH	93	Reserved
32H	50	Reserved	60H	96	Reserved
34H	52	Reserved	61H	97	Reserved
37H	55	Reserved	64H	100	Reserved
50H	80	Reserved			

"Normal" File Control Block

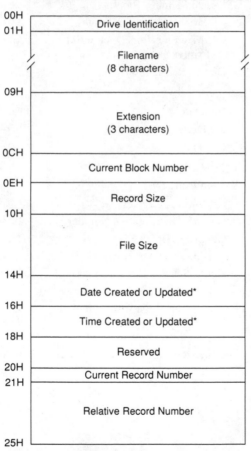

*For format of date and time, see Int 21H Function 57H

Program Segment Prefix (PSP)

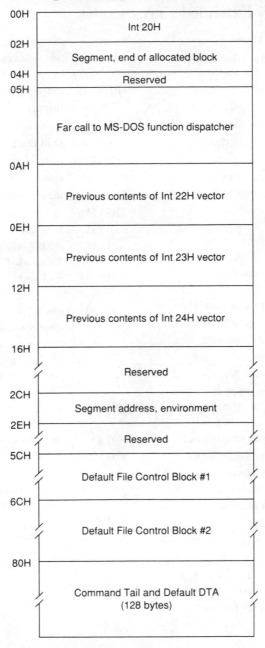

Offset	Contents
00H	Int 20H
02H	Segment, end of allocated block
04H	Reserved
05H	Far call to MS-DOS function dispatcher
0AH	Previous contents of Int 22H vector
0EH	Previous contents of Int 23H vector
12H	Previous contents of Int 24H vector
16H	Reserved
2CH	Segment address, environment
2EH	Reserved
5CH	Default File Control Block #1
6CH	Default File Control Block #2
80H	Command Tail and Default DTA (128 bytes)

MS-DOS Extended Error Codes

Value	Meaning	Value	Meaning
01H	function number invalid	1AH (26)	unknown media type
02H	file not found	1BH (27)	sector not found
03H	path not found	1CH (28)	printer out of paper
04H	too many open files	1DH (29)	write fault
05H	access denied	1EH (30)	read fault
06H	handle invalid	1FH (31)	general failure
07H	memory control blocks destroyed	20H (32)	sharing violation
		21H (33)	lock violation
08H	insufficient memory	22H (34)	disk change invalid
		23H (35)	FCB unavailable
09H	memory block address invalid	24H (36)	sharing buffer exceeded
0AH (10)	environment invalid	25H-31H (37-49)	reserved
0BH (11)	format invalid	32H (50)	unsupported network request
0CH (12)	access code invalid		
0DH (13)	data invalid	33H (51)	remote machine not listening
0EH (14)	unknown unit		
0FH (15)	disk drive invalid	34H (52)	duplicate name on network
10H (16)	attempted to remove current directory	35H (53)	network name not found
11H (17)	not same device	36H (54)	network busy
12H (18)	no more files	37H (55)	device no longer exists on network
13H (19)	disk write-protected	38H (56)	netBIOS command limit exceeded
14H (20)	unknown unit		
15H (21)	drive not ready	39H (57)	error in network adapter hardware
16H (22)	unknown command		
17H (23)	data error (CRC)	3AH (58)	incorrect response from network
18H (24)	bad request structure length		
19H (25)	seek error	3BH (59)	unexpected network error

(continued)

MS-DOS Extended Error Codes *(cont.)*

Value	Meaning	Value	Meaning
3CH (60)	remote adapter incompatible	47H (71)	network request not accepted
3DH (61)	print queue full	48H (72)	print or disk redirection paused
3EH (62)	queue not full		
3FH (63)	not enough room for print file	49H-4FH (73-79)	reserved
40H (64)	network name deleted	50H (80)	file already exists
		51H (81)	reserved
41H (65)	access denied	52H (82)	cannot make directory
42H (66)	incorrect network device type		
		53H (83)	fail on Int 24H (critical error)
43H (67)	network name not found		
		54H (84)	out of structures
44H (68)	network name limit exceeded	55H (85)	already assigned
		56H (86)	invalid password
45H (69)	netBIOS session limit exceeded	57H (87)	invalid parameter
		58H (88)	net write fault
46H (70)	temporary pause		

Int 20H   [1] [2] [3]
Terminate Process

Terminates the current process. This is one of several methods that a program can use to perform a final exit. MS-DOS then takes the following actions:

- All memory belonging to the process is released.

- File buffers are flushed, and any open handles for files or devices owned by the process are closed.

- The termination handler vector (Int 22H) is restored from PSP:000AH.

- The Ctrl-C handler vector (Int 23H) is restored from PSP:000EH.

- The critical-error handler vector (Int 24H) is restored from PSP:0012H (MS-DOS versions 2.0 and later).

- Control is transferred to the termination handler.

If the program is returning to COMMAND.COM, control transfers to the resident portion, and the transient portion is reloaded if necessary. If a batch file is in progress, the next line of the file is fetched and interpreted; otherwise, a prompt is issued for the next user command.

Call with:

CS   = segment address of program segment prefix

Returns:

Nothing

Notes:

- Any files that have been written to using FCBs should be closed before performing this exit call; otherwise, data may be lost.
- Other methods of performing a final exit are:
  – Int 21H Function 00H
  – Int 21H Function 31H
  – Int 21H Function 4CH
  – Int 27H

- [3] If the program is running on a network, it should remove all locks it has placed on file regions before terminating.
- [2] [3] Int 21H Functions 31H and 4CH are the preferred method for termination because they allow a return code to be passed to the parent process.

Int 21H Function 00H [1] [2] [3]
Terminate Process

Terminates the current process. This is one of several methods that a program can use to perform a final exit. MS-DOS then takes the following actions:

- All memory belonging to the process is released.
- File buffers are flushed and any open handles for files or devices owned by the process are closed.
- The termination handler vector (Int 22H) is restored from PSP:000AH.
- The Ctrl-C handler vector (Int 23H) is restored from PSP:000EH.
- [2] [3] The critical-error handler vector (Int 24H) is restored from PSP:0012H.
- Control is transferred to the termination handler.

If the program is returning to COMMAND.COM, control transfers to the resident portion, and the transient portion is reloaded if necessary. If a batch file is in progress, the next line of the file is fetched and interpreted; otherwise, a prompt is issued for the next user command.

Call with:

AH   = 00H
CS   = segment address of program segment prefix

Returns:

Nothing

Notes:

- Any files that have been written to using FCBs should be closed before performing this exit call; otherwise, data may be lost.

- Other methods of performing a final exit are:
  – Int 20H
  – Int 21H Function 31H
  – Int 21H Function 4CH
  – Int 27H

- [3] If the program is running on a network, it should remove all locks it has placed on file regions before terminating.

- [2] [3] Int 21H Functions 31H and 4CH are the preferred method for termination because they allow a return code to be passed to the parent process.

Int 21H Function 01H   [1] [2] [3]
Character Input with Echo

[1] Inputs a character from the keyboard, then echoes it to the display. If no character is ready, waits until one is available.

[2] [3] Reads a character from the standard input device and echoes it to the standard output device. If no character is ready, waits until one is available. Input can be redirected (if input has been redirected, there is no way to detect EOF).

Call with:

AH   = 01H

Returns:

AL   = 8-bit input data

Notes:

■ If the standard input is not redirected and the character read is a
  Ctrl-C, an Int 23H is executed. If the standard input is redirected, a
  Ctrl-C is detected at the console; and if BREAK is ON, an Int 23H
  is executed.

■ To read extended ASCII codes (such as the special function keys
  F1 to F10) on the IBM PC and compatibles, you must call this function twice. The first call returns the value 00H to signal the presence of an extended code.

■ See also Int 21H Functions 06H, 07H, and 08H, which provide
  character input with various combinations of echo and/or Ctrl-C
  sensing.

■ [2] [3] You can also read the keyboard by issuing a read (Int 21H
  Function 3FH) using the predefined handle for the standard input
  (0000H), if input has not been redirected, or a handle obtained by
  opening the logical device CON.

Int 21H Function 02H   [1] [2] [3]
Character Output

[1] Outputs a character to the currently active video display.

[2] [3] Outputs a character to the standard output device. Output can
be redirected (if output is redirected, there is no way to detect disk
full).

Call with:

AH   = 02H
DL   = 8-bit data for output

Returns:

Nothing

Notes:

■ If a Ctrl-C is detected at the keyboard after the requested character
  is output, an Int 23H is executed.

- If the standard output has not been redirected, a backspace code (08H) causes the cursor to move left one position. If output has been redirected, the backspace code does not receive any special treatment.

- [2] [3] You can also send strings to the display by performing a write (Int 21H Function 40H) using the predefined handle for the standard output (0001H), if output has not been redirected, or a handle obtained by opening the logical device CON.

Int 21H Function 03H [1] [2] [3]
Auxiliary Input

[1] Reads a character from the first serial port.

[2] [3] Reads a character from the standard auxiliary device. The default is the first serial port (COM1).

Call with:

    AH   = 03H

Returns:

    AL   − 8-bit input data

Notes:

- In most MS-DOS systems, the serial device is unbuffered and is not interrupt driven. If the auxiliary device sends data faster than your program can process it, characters may be lost.

- At startup on the IBM PC, PC-DOS initializes the first serial port to 2400 baud, no parity, 1 stop bit, and 8 data bits. Other implementations of MS-DOS may initialize the serial device differently.

- There is no way for a user program to read the status of the auxiliary device or to detect I/O errors (such as lost characters) through this function call. On the IBM PC, more precise control may be obtained by calling ROM BIOS Int 14H or by driving the communications controller directly.

- If a Ctrl-C is detected at the keyboard, an Int 23H is executed.

- [2] [3] You can also input from the auxiliary device by requesting a read (Int 21H Function 3FH) using the predefined handle for the standard auxiliary device (0003H) or using a handle obtained by opening the logical device AUX.

Int 21H Function 04H [1] [2] [3]
Auxiliary Output

[1] Outputs a character to the first serial port.

[2] [3] Outputs a character to the standard auxiliary device. The default is the first serial port (COM1).

Call with:

> AH   = 04H
> DL   = 8-bit data for output

Returns:

> Nothing

Notes:

- If the output device is busy, this function waits until the device is ready to accept a character.

- There is no way to poll the status of the auxiliary device using this function. On the IBM PC, more precise control can be obtained by calling ROM BIOS Int 14H or by driving the communications controller directly.

- If a Ctrl-C is detected at the keyboard, an Int 23H is executed.

- [2] [3] You can also send strings to the auxiliary device by performing a write (Int 21H Function 40H) using the predefined handle for the standard auxiliary device (0003H) or using a handle obtained by opening the logical device AUX.

Int 21H Function 05H [1] [2] [3]
Printer Output

[1] Sends a character to the first list device (PRN or LPT1).

[2] [3] Sends a character to the standard list device. The default is the printer on the first parallel port (LPT1), unless explicitly redirected by the user with the MODE command.

Call with:

> AH   = 05H
> DL   = 8-bit data for output

Returns:

Nothing

Notes:

- If the printer is busy, this function waits until the printer is ready to accept the character.

- There is no standardized way to poll the status of the printer under MS-DOS.

- If a Ctrl-C is detected at the keyboard, an Int 23H is executed.

- [2] [3] You can also send strings to the printer by performing a write (Int 21H Function 40H) using the predefined handle for the standard printer device (0004H) or using a handle obtained by opening the logical device PRN or LPT1.

Int 21H Function 06H [1] [2] [3]
Direct Console I/O

Used by programs that need to read and write all possible characters and control codes without any interference from the operating system.

[1] Reads a character from the keyboard or writes a character to the display.

[2] [3] Reads a character from the standard input device or writes a character to the standard output device. I/O may be redirected (if I/O has been redirected, there is no way to detect EOF or disk full).

Call with:

AH	= 06H
DL	= function requested
	00H-FEH *if output request*
	0FFH *if input request*

Returns:

If called with DL=00H-0FEH
Nothing

If called with DL=FFH and a character is ready
Zero flag = clear
AL = 8-bit input data

If called with DL=FFH and no character is ready
Zero flag = set

Notes:

- No special action is taken upon entry of a Ctrl-C when this service is used.

- To read extended ASCII codes (such as the special function keys F1 to F10) on the IBM PC and compatibles, you must call this function twice. The first call returns the value 00H to signal the presence of an extended code.

- See also Int 21H Functions 01H, 07H, and 08H, which provide character input with various combinations of echo and/or Ctrl-C sensing, and Functions 02H and 09H, which may be used to write characters to the standard output.

- [2] [3] You can also read the keyboard by issuing a read (Int 21H Function 3FH) using the predefined handle for the standard input (0000H), if input has not been redirected, or a handle obtained by opening the logical device CON.

- [2] [3] You can also send characters to the display by issuing a write (Int 21H Function 40H) using the predefined handle for the standard output (0001H), if output has not been redirected, or a handle obtained by opening the logical device CON.

Int 21H Function 07H [1] [2] [3]
Unfiltered Character Input Without Echo

[1] Reads a character from the keyboard without echoing it to the display. If no character is ready, waits until one is available.

[2] [3] Reads a character from the standard input device without echoing it to the standard output device. If no character is ready, waits until one is available. Input may be redirected (if input has been redirected, there is no way to detect EOF).

Call with:

AH = 07H

Returns:

AL = 8-bit input data

Notes:

- No special action is taken upon entry of a Ctrl-C when this function is used. If Ctrl-C checking is required, use Int 21H Function 08H instead.

- To read extended ASCII codes (such as the special function keys F1 to F10) on the IBM PC and compatibles, you must call this function twice. The first call returns the value 00H to signal the presence of an extended code.

- See also Int 21H Functions 01H, 06H, and 08H, which provide character input with various combinations of echo and/or Ctrl-C sensing.

- [2] [3] You can also read the keyboard by issuing a read (Int 21H Function 3FH) using the predefined handle for the standard input (0000H), if input has not been redirected, or a handle obtained by opening the logical device CON.

Int 21H Function 08H   [1] [2] [3]
Character Input Without Echo

[1] Reads a character from the keyboard without echoing it to the display. If no character is ready, waits until one is available.

[2] [3] Reads a character from the standard input device without echoing it to the standard output device. If no character is ready, waits until one is available. Input may be redirected (if input has been redirected, there is no way to detect EOF).

Call with:

    AH   = 08H

Returns:

    AL   = 8-bit input data

Notes:

- If the standard input is not redirected, and the character read is a Ctrl-C, an Int 23H is executed. If the standard input is redirected, a Ctrl-C is detected at the console, and BREAK is ON, an Int 23H is executed. To avoid possible interruption by a Ctrl-C, use Int 21H Function 07H instead.

- To read extended ASCII codes (such as the special function keys F1 to F10) on the IBM PC and compatibles, you must call this function twice. The first call returns the value 00H to signal the presence of an extended code.

- See also Int 21H Functions 01H, 06H, and 07H, which provide character input with various combinations of echo and/or Ctrl-C sensing.

- [2] [3] You can also read the keyboard by issuing a read (Int 21H Function 3FH) using the predefined handle for the standard input (0000H), if input has not been redirected, or a handle obtained by opening the logical device CON.

Int 21H Function 09H   [1] [2] [3]
Display String

[1] Sends a string of characters to the display.

[2] [3] Sends a string of characters to the standard output device. Output may be redirected (if output has been redirected, there is no way to detect disk full).

Call with:

AH	= 09H
DS:DX	= segment:offset of string

Returns:

Nothing

Notes:

- The string must be terminated with the character $ (24H), which is not transmitted. Any other ASCII codes, including control codes, can be embedded in the string.

- See Int 21H Functions 02H and 06H for single-character output to the video display or standard output device.

- If a Ctrl-C is detected at the keyboard, an Int 23H is executed.

- [2] [3] You can also send strings to the display by performing a write (Int 21H Function 40H) using the predefined handle for the standard output (0001H), if it has not been redirected, or a handle obtained by opening the logical device CON.

Int 21H Function 0AH (10)   [1] [2] [3]
Buffered Keyboard Input

[1] Reads a line from the keyboard and places it in a user-designated buffer. The characters are echoed to the display.

[2] [3] Reads a string of bytes from the standard input device, up to and including an ASCII carriage return (0DH), and places them in a user-designated buffer. The characters are echoed to the standard output device. Input may be redirected (if input has been redirected, there is no way to detect EOF).

Call with:

AH = 0AH
DS:DX = segment:offset of buffer

Returns:

Nothing

Notes:

■ The buffer used by this function has the following format:

Byte	*Contents*
0	maximum number of characters to read, set by program
1	number of characters actually read (excluding carriage return), set by MS-DOS
2+	string read from keyboard or standard input, terminated by a carriage return (0DH)

■ If the buffer fills to one fewer than the maximum number of characters it can hold, subsequent input is ignored and the bell is sounded until a carriage return is detected.

■ This input function is buffered with type-ahead capability, and all of the standard keyboard editing commands are active.

■ If the standard input is not redirected, and a Ctrl-C is detected at the console, an Int 23H is executed. If the standard input is redirected, a Ctrl-C is detected at the console, and BREAK is ON, an Int 23H is executed.

■ See Int 21H Functions 01H, 06H, 07H, and 08H for single-character input from the keyboard or standard input device.

■ [2] [3] You can also read strings from the keyboard by performing a read (Int 21H Function 3FH) using the predefined handle for the standard input (0000H), if it has not been redirected, or a handle obtained by opening the logical device CON.

Int 21H Function 0BH (11) [1] [2] [3]
Check Input Status

[1] Checks whether a character is available from the keyboard.

[2] [3] Checks whether a character is available from the standard input device. Input can be redirected.

Call with:

AH   = 0BH

Returns:

AL   = 00H if no character is available
           FFH if at least one character is available

Notes:

- If a Ctrl-C is detected, an Int 23H is executed.

- If the standard input is not redirected, and a Ctrl-C is detected at the console, an Int 23H is executed. If the standard input is redirected, a Ctrl-C is detected at the console, and BREAK is ON, an Int 23H is executed.

- If a character is waiting, this function will continue to return a true flag until the character is consumed with a call to Int 21H Function 01H, 06H, 07H, 08H, 0AH, or 3FH.

- This function is equivalent to IOCTL Int 21H Function 44H Subfunction 06H.

Int 21H Function 0CH (12) [1] [2] [3]
Flush Input Buffer and Then Input

[1] Clears the type-ahead buffer and then invokes one of the keyboard input functions.

[2] [3] Clears the standard input buffer and then invokes one of the character input functions. Input can be redirected.

Call with:

AH   = 0CH
AL   = number of input function to be invoked after reset-
           ting buffer (must be 01H, 06H, 07H, 08H, or 0AH)

(if AL = 0AH)
DS:DX   = segment:offset of input buffer

Returns:

If called with AL = 01H, 06H, 07H, or 08H
AL   = 8-bit input data

If called with AL = 0AH
Nothing

Notes:

■ The function exists to allow a program to defeat MS-DOS's
type-ahead feature. It discards any characters that are waiting in
MS-DOS's internal type-ahead buffer, forcing the specified input
function to wait for a character (usually a keyboard entry) that is
truly entered after the program's request.

■ The presence or absence of Ctrl-C checking during execution of
this function depends on the function number in register AL.

■ A function number in AL other than 01H, 06H, 07H, 08H, or 0AH
simply flushes the input buffer and returns control to the calling
program.

Int 21H Function 0DH (13)   [1] [2] [3]
Disk Reset

Flushes all file buffers. All data that has been logically written by user
programs, but has been temporarily buffered within MS-DOS, is
physically written to the disk.

Call with:

AH   = 0DH

Returns:

Nothing

Notes:

- This function does not update the disk directory for any files that are still open. If your program fails to properly close all files before the disk is removed, and files have changed size, the data forced out to the disk by this function may still be inaccessible because the directory entries will not be correct.

- [3.3] Int 21H Function 68H (Commit File) should be used in preference to this function because it also updates the disk directory and file allocation table.

Int 21H Function 0EH (14)   [1] [2] [3]
Select Disk

Selects the specified drive to be the current, or default, disk drive and returns the total number of logical drives in the system.

Call with:

AH	= 0EH
DL	= drive code (0=A, 1=B, etc.)

Returns:

AL	= number of logical drives in system

Notes:

- [1] 16 drive designators (0 through 0FH) are available.
- [2] 63 drive designators (0 through 3FH) are available.
- [3] 26 drive designators (0 through 19H) are available.
- To preserve upward compatibility, new applications should limit themselves to the drive letters A–Z (0=A, 1=B, etc.).
- *Logical* drives means the total number of block devices: floppy disks, simulated disk drives (RAMdisks), and hard-disk drives. A single physical hard-disk drive is frequently partitioned into two or more logical drives.
- [1] [2] In single-drive IBM PC-compatible systems, the value 2 is returned in AL, because PC-DOS supports two logical drives (A: and B:) on the single physical floppy-disk drive. The actual number of physical drives in the system can be determined with ROM BIOS Int 11H.

- [3] The value returned in AL is either 5 or the drive code corresponding to the LASTDRIVE entry (if any) in CONFIG.SYS, whichever is greater.

Int 21H Function 0FH (15)   [1] [2] [3]
Open File

Opens a file and makes it available for subsequent read/write operations.

Call with:

AH   = 0FH
DS:DX   = segment:offset of file control block

Returns:

If function successful (file found)
AL   = 00

and FCB filled in by MS-DOS as follows:
drive field (offset 00H)   = *1 for drive A, 2 for drive B, etc.*
current block field (offset 0CH)   = *00H*
record size field (offset 0EH)   = *0080H*
[2] [3] size field (offset 10H)   = *file size from directory*
[2] [3] date field (offset 14H)   = *date stamp from directory*
[2] [3] time field (offset 16H)   = *time stamp from directory*

If function unsuccessful (file not found)
AL   = 0FFH

Notes:

- If your program is going to use a record size other than 128 bytes, it should set the record size field at FCB offset 0EH *after* the file is successfully opened and *before* any other disk operation.

- If random access is to be performed, the calling program must also set the FCB relative-record field (offset 21H) after successfully opening the file.

- [3] If the program is running on a network, the file is opened for read/write access in compatibility sharing mode.

- For format of directory time and date, see Int 21H Function 57H.

- [2] [3] Int 21H Function 3DH, which allows full access to the hierarchical directory structure, should be used in preference to this function.

Int 21H Function 10H (16)   [1] [2] [3]
Close File

Closes a file, flushes all MS-DOS internal disk buffers associated
with the file to disk, and updates the disk directory if the file has been
modified or extended.

Call with:

> AH   = 10H
> DS:DX   = segment:offset of file control block

Returns:

> *If function successful (directory update successful)*
> AL   = 00H

> *If function unsuccessful (file not found in directory)*
> AL   = FFH

Notes:

- [2] MS-DOS versions 1.x and 2.x do not reliably detect a disk
  change, and an error can occur if the user changes disks while a
  file is still open on that drive. In the worst case, the directory and
  file allocation table of the newly inserted disk may be damaged or
  destroyed.

- [2] [3] Int 21H Function 3EH should be used in preference to this
  function.

Int 21H Function 11H (17)   [1] [2] [3]
Find First File

Searches the current directory on the designated drive for a matching
filename.

Call with:

> AH   = 11H
> DS:DX   = segment:offset of file control block

Returns:

If function successful (matching filename found)
AL   = 00H

and buffer at current disk transfer area (DTA) address filled in as an unopened normal FCB or extended FCB, depending on which type of FCB was input to function

If function unsuccessful (no matching filename found)
AL   = FFH

Notes:

- It is important to use Int 21H Function 1AH to set the DTA to point to a buffer of adequate size before using this function call.

- The wildcard character ? is allowed in the filename in all versions of MS-DOS. In versions 3.0 and later, the wildcard character * may also be used in a filename. If ? or * is used, this function returns the first matching filename.

- An extended FCB must be used to search for files that have the system, hidden, read-only, directory, or volume-label attributes.

- If an extended FCB is used, its attribute byte determines the type of search that will be performed. If the attribute byte (byte 0) contains 00H, only ordinary files are found. If the volume-label attribute bit is set, only volume labels will be returned (if any are present). If any other attribute or combination of attributes is set (such as hidden, system, or read-only), those files and all ordinary files will be matched.

- [2] [3] Int 21H Function 4EH, which allows full access to the hierarchical directory structure, should be used in preference to this function.

Int 21H Function 12H (18)   [1] [2] [3]
Find Next File

Given that a previous call to Int 21H Function 11H has been successful, returns the next matching filename (if any).

Call with:

AH   = 12H
DS:DX   = segment:offset of file control block

Returns:

If function successful (matching filename found)
AL   = 00H

and buffer at current disk transfer area (DTA) address set up as an
unopened normal FCB or extended FCB, depending on which type
of FCB was originally input to Int 21H Function 11H

If function unsuccessful (no more matching filenames found)
AL   = FFH

Notes:

- This function assumes that the FCB used as input has been properly initialized by a previous call to Int 21H Function 11H (and
  possible subsequent calls to Int 21H Function 12H) and that the
  filename or extension being searched for contained at least one
  wildcard character.

- As with Int 21H Function 11H, it is important to use Int 21H Function 1AH to set the DTA to a buffer of adequate size before using
  this function.

- [2] [3] Int 21H Functions 4EH and 4FH, which allow full access to
  the hierarchical directory structure, should be used in preference to
  this function.

Int 21H Function 13H (19)   [1] [2] [3]
Delete File

Deletes all matching files from the current directory on the default or
specified disk drive.

Call with:

AH   = 13H
DS:DX   = segment:offset of file control block

Returns:

If function successful (file or files deleted)
AL   = 00H

*If function unsuccessful (no matching files were found, or at least
one matching file was read-only)*
AL   = FFH

Notes:

- The wildcard character ? is allowed in the filename; if ? is present and there is more than one matching filename, all matching files will be deleted.

- [3] If the program is running on a network, the user must have Create rights to the directory containing the file to be deleted.

- [2] [3] Int 21H Function 41H, which allows full access to the hierarchical directory structure, should be used in preference to this function.

Int 21H Function 14H (20)   [1] [2] [3]
Sequential Read

Reads the next sequential block of data from a file and then increments the file pointer appropriately.

Call with:

AH	= 14H
DS:DX	= segment:offset of previously opened file control block

Returns:

AL	= 00H	if read successful
	01H	if end of file
	02H	if segment wrap
	03H	if partial record read at end of file

Notes:

- The record is read into memory at the current disk transfer area (DTA) address, specified by the most recent call to Int 21H Function 1AH. If the size of the record and the location of the buffer are such that a segment overflow or wraparound would occur, the function fails with a return code of 02H.

- The number of bytes of data to be read is specified by the record size field (offset 0EH) of the file control block (FCB).

- The file location of the data that will be read is specified by the combination of the current block field (offset 0CH) and current record field (offset 20H) of the file control block (FCB). These fields are also automatically incremented by this function.

- If a partial record is read at the end of file, it is padded to the requested record length with zeros.

- [3] If the program is running on a network, the user must have Read access rights to the directory containing the file to be read.

Int 21H Function 15H (21) [1] [2] [3]
Sequential Write

Writes the next sequential block of data into a file and then increments the file pointer appropriately.

Call with:

AH   = 15H
DS:DX   = segment:offset of previously opened file control block

Returns:

AL   = 00H   if write successful
         01H   if disk is full
         02H   if segment wrap

Notes:

- The record is written (logically, not necessarily physically) to the disk from memory at the current disk transfer area (DTA) address, specified by the most recent call to Int 21H Function 1AH. If the size of the record and the location of the buffer are such that a segment overflow or wraparound would occur, the function fails with a return code of 02H.

- The number of bytes of data to be written is specified by the record size field (offset 0EH) of the file control block (FCB).

- The file location of the data that will be written is specified by the combination of the current block field (offset 0CH) and current record field (offset 20H) of the file control block (FCB). These fields are also automatically incremented by this function.

- [3] If the program is running on a network, the user must have Write access rights to the directory containing the file to be written.

Int 21H Function 16H (22)   [1] [2] [3]
Create File

Creates a new directory entry in the current directory or truncates any existing file with the same name to zero length. Opens the file for subsequent read/write operations.

Call with:

AH   = 16H
DS:DX   = segment:offset of unopened file control block

Returns:

If function successful (file was created or truncated)
AL   = 00H

and FCB filled in by MS-DOS as follows:

drive field (offset 00H)	*= 1 for drive A, 2 for drive B, etc.*
current block field (offset 0CH)	*= 00H*
record size field (offset 0EH)	*= 0080H*
[2] [3] size field (offset 10H)	*= file size from directory*
[2] [3] date field (offset 14H)	*= date stamp from directory*
[2] [3] time field (offset 16H)	*= time stamp from directory*

If function unsuccessful (directory full)
AL   = FFH

Notes:

■ Since an existing file with the specified name is truncated to zero length (i.e., all data in that file is irretrievably lost), this function must be used with caution.

■ If this function is called with an extended file control block (FCB), the new file may be assigned a special attribute such as hidden or system during its creation by setting the appropriate bit in the extended FCB's attribute byte.

■ Since this function also opens the file, a subsequent call to Int 21H Function 0FH is not required.

■ [3] If the program is running on a network, the user must have Create rights to the directory that will contain the new file.

■ For format of directory time and date, see Int 21H Function 57H.

■ [2] [3] Int 21H Functions 3CH, 5AH, and 5BH, which provide full access to the hierarchical directory structure, should be used in preference to this function.

Int 21H Function 17H (23) [1] [2] [3]
Rename File

Alters the name of all matching files in the current directory on the disk in the specified drive.

Call with:

AH = 17H
DS:DX = segment:offset of "special" file control block

Returns:

If function successful (one or more files renamed)
AL = 00H

If function unsuccessful (no matching files, or new filename matched an existing file)
AL = FFH

Notes:

- The special file control block has a drive code, filename, and extension in the usual position (bytes 0 through 0BH) and a second filename starting 6 bytes after the first (offset 11H).

- The *?* wildcard character can be used in the first filename. Every file matching the first file specification will be renamed to match the second file specification.

- If the second file specification contains any *?* wildcard characters, the corresponding letters in the first filename are left unchanged.

- The function terminates if the new name to be assigned to a file matches that of an existing file.

- [2] [3] An extended FCB can be used with this function to rename a directory.

- [2] [3] Int 21H Function 56H, which allows full access to the hierarchical directory structure, should be used in preference to this function.

Int 21H Function 18H (24) [1] [2] [3]
Reserved

Int 21H Function 19H (25) [1] [2] [3]
Get Current Disk

Returns the drive code of the current, or default, disk drive.

Call with:

    AH   = 19H

Returns:

    AL   = drive code (0=A, 1=B, etc.)

Notes:

- To set the default drive, use Int 21H Function 0EH.

- Some other Int 21H functions use drive codes beginning at 1 (that is, 1=A, 2=B, etc.) and reserve drive code zero for the default drive.

Int 21H Function 1AH (26) [1] [2] [3]
Set DTA Address

Specifies the address of the disk transfer area (DTA) to be used for subsequent FCB-related function calls.

Call with:

    AH   = 1AH
    DS:DX   = segment:offset of disk transfer area

Returns:

    Nothing

Notes:

- If this function is never called by the program, the DTA defaults to a 128-byte buffer at offset 0080H in the program segment prefix.

- In general, it is the programmer's responsibility to ensure that the buffer area specified is large enough for any disk operation that will use it. The only exception to this is that MS-DOS will detect and abort disk transfers that would cause a segment wrap.

- Int 21H Function 2FH can be used to determine the current disk transfer address.

- The only handle-type operations that rely on the current DTA address are the directory search functions, Int 21H Functions 4EH and 4FH.

Int 21H Function 1BH (27)   [1] [2] [3]
Get Default Drive Data

Obtains selected information about the default disk drive and a pointer to the media identification byte from its file allocation table.

Call with:

AH   = 1BH

Returns:

If function successful
AL   = sectors per cluster
DS:BX   = segment:offset of media ID byte
CX   = size of physical sector (bytes)
DX   = number of clusters for default drive

If function unsuccessful (invalid drive or critical error)
AL   = FFH

Notes:

- The media ID byte has the following meanings:

0F0H	3.5-inch double-sided, 18 sectors or "other"
0F8H	fixed disk
0F9H	5.25-inch double-sided, 15 sectors or 3.5-inch double-sided, 9 sectors
0FCH	5.25-inch single-sided, 9 sectors
0FDH	5.25-inch double-sided, 9 sectors
0FEH	5.25-inch single-sided, 8 sectors
0FFH	5.25-inch double-sided, 8 sectors

- To obtain information about disks other than the one in the default drive, use Int 21H Function 1CH or 36H.

- [1] The address returned in DS:BX points to a copy of the first sector of the actual FAT, with the media ID byte in the first byte.

- [2] [3] The address returned in DS:BX points only to a copy of the media ID byte from the disk's FAT; the memory above that address cannot be assumed to contain the FAT or any other useful information. If direct access to the FAT is required, use Int 25H to read it into memory.

Int 21H Function 1CH (28) [2] [3]
Get Drive Data

Obtains allocation information about the specified disk drive and a
pointer to the media identification byte from its file allocation table.

Call with:

AH = 1CH
DL = drive code (0=default, 1=A, etc.)

Returns:

If function successful
AL = sectors per cluster
DS:BX = segment:offset of media ID byte
CX = size of physical sector (bytes)
DX = number of clusters for default or specified drive

If function unsuccessful (invalid drive or critical error)
AL = FFH

Notes:

■ The media ID byte has the following meanings:

0F0H	3.5-inch double-sided, 18 sectors or ''other''
0F8H	fixed disk
0F9H	5.25-inch double-sided, 15 sectors or 3.5-inch double-sided, 9 sectors
0FCH	5.25-inch single-sided, 9 sectors
0FDH	5.25-inch double-sided, 9 sectors
0FEH	5.25-inch single-sided, 8 sectors
0FFH	5.25-inch double-sided, 8 sectors

■ In general, this call is identical to Int 21H Function 1BH, except for
the ability to designate a specific disk drive. See also Int 21H Function 36H, which returns similar information.

■ [1] The address returned in DS:BX points to a copy of the first sector of the actual FAT, with the media ID byte in the first byte.

■ [2] [3] The address returned in DS:BX points only to a copy of the
media ID byte from the disk's FAT; the memory above that address
cannot be assumed to contain the FAT or any other useful information. If direct access to the FAT is required, use Int 25H to read it
into memory.

Int 21H Function 1DH (29)   [1] [2] [3]
Reserved

Int 21H Function 1EH (30)   [1] [2] [3]
Reserved

Int 21H Function 1FH (31)   [1] [2] [3]
Reserved

Int 21H Function 20H (32)   [1] [2] [3]
Reserved

Int 21H Function 21H (33)   [1] [2] [3]
Random Read

Reads a selected record from a file into memory.

Call with:

AH	= 21H
DS:DX	= segment:offset of previously opened file control block

Returns:

AL	= 00H	if read successful
	01H	if end of file
	02H	if segment wrap, read canceled
	03H	if partial record read at end of file

Notes:

■ The record is read into memory at the current disk transfer area address, specified by the most recent call to Int 21H Function 1AH. It is the programmer's responsibility to ensure that this area is large enough for any record that will be transferred. If the size and location of the buffer are such that a segment overflow or wraparound would occur, the function fails with a return code of 02H.

■ The file location of the data to be read is determined by the combination of the relative-record field (offset 21H) and the record size field (offset 0EH) of the FCB. The default record size is 128 bytes.

■ The current block field (offset 0CH) and current record field (offset 20H) are updated to agree with the relative-record field as a side effect of the function.

■ The relative-record field of the FCB is not incremented by this function; it is the responsibility of the application to update the FCB appropriately if it wishes to read successive records. Compare with Int 21H Function 27H, which can read multiple records with one function call and automatically increments the relative-record field.

■ If a partial record is read at end of file, it is padded to the requested record length with zeros.

■ [3] If the program is running on a network, the user must have Read access rights to the directory containing the file to be read.

Int 21H Function 22H (34)   [1] [2] [3]
Random Write

Writes data from memory into a selected record in a file.

Call with:

AH	= 22H
DS:DX	= segment:offset of previously opened file control block

Returns:

AL	= 00H	if write successful
	01H	if disk full
	02H	if segment wrap, write canceled

Notes:

■ The record is written (logically, not necessarily physically) to the file from memory at the current disk transfer address, specified by the most recent call to Int 21H Function 1AH. If the size and location of the buffer are such that a segment overflow or wraparound would occur, the function fails with a return code of 02H.

■ The file location of the data to be written is determined by the combination of the relative-record field (offset 21H) and the record size field (offset 0EH) of the FCB. The default record size is 128 bytes.

■ The current block field (offset 0CH) and current record field (offset 20H) are updated to agree with the relative-record field as a side effect of the function.

■ The relative-record field of the FCB is not incremented by this function; it is the responsibility of the application to update the FCB appropriately if it wishes to write successive records. Compare with Int 21H Function 28H, which can write multiple records with one function call and automatically increments the relative-record field.

■ If a record is written beyond the current end of file, the space between the old end of file and the new record is allocated but not initialized.

■ [3] If the program is running on a network, the user must have Write access rights to the directory containing the file to be written.

Int 21H Function 23H (35)　　[1] [2] [3]
Get File Size

Searches for a matching file in the current directory; if one is found, updates the FCB with the file's size in terms of number of records.

Call with:

    AH   = 23H
    DS:DX   = segment:offset of unopened file control block

Returns:

If function successful (matching file found)
AL   = 00

and FCB relative-record field (offset 21H) set to the number of records in the file, rounded up if necessary to the next complete record

If function unsuccessful (no matching file found)
AL   = FFH

Notes:

■ An appropriate value must be placed in the FCB record size field (offset 0EH) *before* calling this function. There is no default record size for this function. Compare with the FCB-related open and create functions (Int 21H Functions 0FH and 16H), which initialize the FCB for a default record size of 128 bytes.

■ The record size field can be set to 1 to find the size of the file in bytes.

■ Because record numbers are zero based, this function can be used to position the FCB's file pointer to the end of file.

Int 21H Function 24H (36)   [1] [2] [3]
Set Relative Record Number

Sets the relative-record number field of a file control block (FCB) to correspond to the current file position as recorded in the opened FCB.

Call with:

AH   = 24H
DS:DX   = segment:offset of previously opened file control
               block

Returns:

AL is destroyed (other registers not affected)

FCB relative-record field (offset 21H) updated

Notes:

■ This function is used when switching from sequential to random I/O within a file. The contents of the relative-record field (offset

21H) are derived from the record size (offset 0EH), current block (offset 0CH), and current record (offset 20H) fields of the file control block.

- All four bytes of the FCB relative-record field (offset 21H) should be initialized to zero before calling this function.

Int 21H Function 25H (37)   [1] [2] [3]
Set Interrupt Vector

Initializes a machine interrupt vector to point to an interrupt handling routine.

Call with:

AH	= 25H
AL	= interrupt number
DS:DX	= segment:offset of interrupt handling routine

Returns:

Nothing

Notes:

- This function should be used in preference to direct editing of the interrupt vector table by well-behaved applications.
- Before an interrupt vector is modified, its original value should be obtained with Int 21H Function 35H and saved so that it can be restored using this function before program termination.

Int 21H Function 26H (38)   [1] [2] [3]
Create New PSP

Copies the program segment prefix (PSP) of the currently executing program to a specified segment address in free memory and then updates the new PSP to make it usable by another program.

Call with:

AH	= 26H
DX	= segment of new program segment prefix

Returns:

Nothing

Notes:

■ After the executing program's PSP is copied into the new segment, the memory size information in the new PSP is updated appropriately and the current contents of the termination (Int 22H), Ctrl-C handler (Int 23H), and critical-error handler (Int 24H) vectors are saved starting at offset 0AH.

■ This function does not load another program or in itself cause one to be executed.

■ [2] [3] Int 21H Function 4BH (EXEC), which can be used to load and execute programs or overlays in either .COM or .EXE format, should be used in preference to this function.

Int 21H Function 27H (39) [1] [2] [3]
Random Block Read

Reads one or more sequential records from a file into memory, starting at a designated file location.

Call with:

AH	= 27H
CX	= number of records to read
DS:DX	= segment:offset of previously opened file control block

Returns:

AL	= 00H	if all requested records read
	01H	if end of file
	02H	if segment wrap
	03H	if partial record read at end of file
CX	= actual number of records read	

Notes:

■ The records are read into memory at the current disk transfer area address, specified by the most recent call to Int 21H Function 1AH. It is the programmer's responsibility to ensure that this area is large enough for the group of records that will be transferred. If the size and location of the buffer are such that a segment overflow or wraparound would occur, the function fails with a return code of 02H.

■ The file location of the data to be read is determined by the combination of the relative-record field (offset 21H) and the record size field (offset 0EH) of the FCB. The default record size is 128 bytes.

■ After the disk transfer is performed, the current block (offset 0CH), current record (offset 020H), and relative-record (offset 21H) fields of the FCB are updated to point to the next record in the file.

■ If a partial record is read at the end of file, the remainder of the record is padded with zeros.

■ [3] If the program is running on a network, the user must have Read access rights to the directory containing the file to be read.

■ Compare with Int 21H Function 21H, which transfers only one record per function call and does not update the FCB relative-record field.

Int 21H Function 28H (40)   [1] [2] [3]
Random Block Write

Writes one or more sequential records from memory to a file, starting at a designated file location.

Call with:

AH	= 28H
CX	= number of records to write
DS:DX	= segment:offset of previously opened file control block

Returns:

AL	= 00H	if all requested records written
	01H	if disk full
	02H	if segment wrap
CX	= actual number of records written	

Notes:

■ The records are written (logically, not necessarily physically) to disk from memory at the current disk transfer area address, specified by the most recent call to Int 21H Function 1AH. If the size and location of the buffer are such that a segment overflow or wraparound would occur, the function fails with a return code of 02H.

■ The file location of the data to be written is determined by the combination of the relative-record field (offset 21H) and the record size field (offset 0EH) of the FCB. The default record size is 128 bytes.

■ After the disk transfer is performed, the current block (offset 0CH), current record (offset 020H), and relative-record (offset 21H) fields of the FCB are updated to point to the next record in the file.

■ If this function is called with CX = 00H, no data is written to the disk but the file is extended or truncated to the length specified by combination of the record size (offset 0EH) and the relative-record (offset 21H) fields of the FCB.

■ [3] If the program is running on a network, the user must have Write access rights to the directory containing the file to be written.

■ Compare with Int 21H Function 22H, which transfers only one record per function call and does not update the FCB relative-record field.

Int 21H Function 29H (41)   [1] [2] [3]
Parse Filename

Parses a text string into the various fields of a file control block (FCB).

Call with:

AH	= 29H
AL	= flags to control parsing

    Bit 3 = 1   if extension field in FCB will be modified only if an extension is specified in the string being parsed.

          = 0   if extension field in FCB will be modified regardless; if no extension is present in the parsed string, FCB extension is set to ASCII blanks.

Bit 2	= 1	if filename field in FCB will be modified only if a filename is specified in the string being parsed.
	= 0	if filename field in FCB will be modified regardless; if no filename is present in the parsed string, FCB filename is set to ASCII blanks.
Bit 1	= 1	if drive ID byte in FCB will be modified only if a drive was specified in the string being parsed.
	= 0	if the drive ID byte in FCB will be modified regardless; if no drive specifier is present in the parsed string, FCB drive-code field is set to 0 (default).
Bit 0	= 1	if leading separators will be scanned off (ignored).
	= 0	if leading separators will not be scanned off.
DS:SI		= segment:offset of text string
ES:DI		= segment:offset of file control block

Returns:

AL	= 00H	if no wildcard characters encountered
	01H	if parsed string contained wildcard characters
	FFH	if drive specifier invalid
DS:SI		= segment:offset of first character after parsed filename
ES:DI		= segment:offset of formatted unopened file control block

Notes:

- This function regards the following as separator characters:
  [1] : . ; , = + tab space / " [ ]
  [2] [3] : . ; , = + tab space

- This function regards all control characters and the following as terminator characters:
  : . ; , = + tab space < > ; / " [ ]

- If no valid filename is present in the string to be parsed, upon return ES:DI+1 points to an ASCII blank.

- If the * wildcard character occurs in a filename or extension, it and all remaining characters in the corresponding field in the FCB are set to ?.

- This function (and file control blocks in general) cannot be used with file specifications that include a path.

Int 21H Function 2AH (42)   [1] [2] [3]
Get Date

Obtains the system day of the month, day of the week, month, and year.

Call with:

AH	= 2AH

Returns:

CX	= year (1980 through 2099)
DH	= month (1 through 12)
DL	= day (1 through 31)

Under MS-DOS versions 1.1 and later

AL	= day of the week (0=Sunday, 1=Monday, etc.)

Notes:

- This function's register format is the same as that required for Int 21H Function 2BH (Set Date).

- This function can be used together with Int 21H Function 2BH to find the day of the week for an arbitrary date. The current date is first obtained with Function 2AH and saved. The date of interest is then set with Function 2BH, and the day of the week for that date is obtained with a subsequent call to Function 2AH. Finally, the current date is restored with an additional call to Function 2BH, using the values obtained with the original Function 2AH call.

Int 21H Function 2BH (43)   [1] [2] [3]
Set Date

Initializes the system clock driver to a specific date. The system time is not affected.

AH	= 2BH
CX	= year (1980 through 2099)
DH	= month (1 through 12)
DL	= day (1 through 31)

Returns:

AL	= 00H	if date set successfully
	FFH	if date not valid (ignored)

Note:

- This function's register format is the same as that required for Int 21H Function 2AH (Get Date).

Int 21H Function 2CH (44)   [1] [2] [3]
Get Time

Obtains the time of day from the system real-time clock driver, converted to hours, minutes, seconds, and hundredths of seconds.

Call with:

AH	= 2CH

Returns:

CH	= hours (0 through 23)
CL	= minutes (0 through 59)
DH	= seconds (0 through 59)
DL	= hundredths of seconds (0 through 99)

Notes:

- This function's register format is the same as that required for Int 21H Function 2DH (Set Time).

- On most IBM PC-compatible systems, the real-time clock does not have a resolution of single hundredths of seconds. On such machines, the values returned by this function in register DL are discontinuous.

Int 21H Function 2DH (45) Set Time

Initializes the system real-time clock to a specified hour, minute, second, and hundredth of second. The system date is not affected.

Call with:

AH	= 2DH
CH	= hours (0 through 23)
CL	= minutes (0 through 59)
DH	= seconds (0 through 59)
DL	= hundredths of seconds (0 through 99)

Returns:

AL	= 00H	if time set successfully
	FFH	if time not valid (ignored)

Note:

■ This function's register format is the same as that required for Int 21H Function 2CH (Get Time).

Int 21H Function 2EH (46) Set Verify Flag

Turns off or turns on the operating-system flag for automatic read-after-write verification of data.

Call with:

AH	= 2EH	
AL	= 00H	if turning off verify flag
	01H	if turning on verify flag
[1] [2]		
DL	= 00H	

Returns:

Nothing

Notes:

- This function provides increased data integrity by allowing the user to force a read-after-write verify of all data written to the disk, if that capability is supported by the manufacturer's disk driver.

- Because read-after-write verification slows disk operations, the default setting of the verify flag is OFF.

- The current state of the verify flag can be determined using Int 21H Function 54H.

- The state of the verify flag is also controlled by the MS-DOS commands VERIFY OFF and VERIFY ON.

Int 21H Function 2FH (47)   [2] [3]
Get DTA Address

Obtains the current address of the disk transfer area (DTA) for FCB file read/write operations.

Call with:

AH	= 2FH

Returns:

ES:BX	= segment:offset of disk transfer area

Note:

- The disk transfer area address is set with Int 21H Function 1AH. The default DTA is a 128-byte buffer at offset 80H in the program segment prefix.

Int 21H Function 30H (48)   [2] [3]
Get MS-DOS Version Number

Returns the version number of the host MS-DOS operating system. This function is used by application programs to determine the capabilities of their environment.

Call with:

AH	= 30H
AL	= 00H

Returns:

[1]
AL   = 00H

[2] [3]
AL   = major version number (MS-DOS 3.1 = 3, etc.)
AH   = minor version number (MS-DOS 3.1 = 0AH, etc.)
BH   = Original Equipment Manufacturer's (OEM's) serial
             number (OEM dependent — usually 00H for IBM's
             PC-DOS, 0FFH or other values for MS-DOS)
BL:CX   = 24-bit user serial number (optional, OEM dependent)

Notes:

■ Because this function was not defined under MS-DOS 1.x, it should
  always be called with AL = 00. In an MS-DOS 1.x environment,
  AL will be returned unchanged.

■ Care must be taken not to exit in an unacceptable fashion if an
  MS-DOS 1.x environment is detected. For example, Int 21H Function 4CH (Terminate Process with Return Code), Int 21H Function
  40H (Write to File or Device), and the standard error handle are
  not available in MS-DOS 1.x. In such cases a program should display an error message using Int 21H Function 09H and then terminate with Int 20H or Int 21H Function 00H.

Int 21H Function 31H (49)   [2] [3]
Terminate and Stay Resident

Terminates execution of the currently executing program, passing a
return code to the parent process, but reserves part or all of the program's memory so that it will not be overlaid by the next transient
program to be loaded. MS-DOS then takes the following actions:

● Flushes the file buffers and closes any open handles for files or
  devices owned by the process.

● Restores the termination handler vector (Int 22H) from
  PSP:000AH.

● Restores the Ctrl-C handler vector (Int 23H) from PSP:000EH.

● [2] [3] Restores the critical-error handler vector (Int 24H) from
  PSP:0012H.

● Transfers control to the termination handler.

If the program is returning to COMMAND.COM, control transfers to the resident portion, and the transient portion is reloaded if necessary. If a batch file is in progress, the next line of the file is fetched and interpreted; otherwise, a prompt is issued for the next user command.

Call with:

AH	= 31H
AL	= return code
DX	= amount of memory to reserve (in paragraphs)

Returns:

Nothing

Notes:

- This function call is typically used to allow user-written utilities, drivers, or interrupt handlers to be loaded as ordinary .COM or .EXE programs and then remain resident. Subsequent entrance to the code is via a hardware or software interrupt.

- This function attempts to set the initial memory allocation block to the length in paragraphs specified in register DX. If other memory blocks have been requested by the application using Int 21H Function 48H, they will not be released by this function.

- Other methods of performing a final exit are:
  - Int 20H
  - Int 21H Function 00H
  - Int 21H Function 4CH
  - Int 27H

- The return code may be retrieved by a parent process through Int 21H Function 4DH (Get Return Code). It can also be tested in a batch file with an IF ERRORLEVEL statement. By convention, a return code of zero indicates successful execution, and a non-zero return code indicates an error.

- This function should not be called by .EXE programs that are loaded at the high end of the transient program area (i.e., linked with the /HIGH switch) because doing so reserves the memory that is normally used by the transient part of COMMAND.COM. If COMMAND.COM cannot be reloaded, the system will fail.

- [3] If the program is running on a network, it should remove all locks it has placed on file regions before terminating.

- [2] [3] This function should be used in preference to Int 27H because it supports return codes, allows larger amounts of memory to be reserved, and does not require CS to contain the segment of the program segment prefix.

Int 21H Function 32H (50)
Reserved

Int 21H Function 33H (51)
Get or Set Break Flag

Obtains or changes the status of the operating system's Break flag, which influences Ctrl-C checking during function calls.

Call with:

If getting Break flag
AH   = 33H
AL   = 00H

If setting Break flag
AH   = 33H
AL   = 01H
DL   = 00H   if turning Break flag OFF
       01H   if turning Break flag ON

Returns:

DL   = 00H   Break flag is OFF
       01H   Break flag is ON

Notes:

■ When the system Break flag is on, the keyboard is examined for a Ctrl-C entry whenever any operating system input or output is requested; if one is detected, control is transferred to the Ctrl-C handler (Int 23H). When the Break flag is off, MS-DOS only checks for a Ctrl-C entry when executing the traditional character I/O functions (Int 21H Functions 01H through 0CH).

■ The Break flag is not part of the local environment of the currently executing program; it affects all programs. An application that alters the flag should first save the flag's original status and then restore the flag before terminating.

Int 21H Function 34H (52)
Reserved

Int 21H Function 35H (53)
Get Interrupt Vector

Obtains the address of the current interrupt handler routine for the specified machine interrupt.

Call with:

AH	= 35H
AL	= interrupt number

Returns:

ES:BX	= segment:offset of interrupt handler

Note:

- Together with Int 21H Function 25H (Set Interrupt Vector), this function is used by well-behaved application programs to modify or inspect the machine interrupt vector table.

Int 21H Function 36H (54)
Get Drive Allocation Information

[2] [3]

Obtains selected information about a disk drive, from which the drive's capacity and remaining free space can be calculated.

Call with:

AH	= 36H
DL	= drive code (0=default, 1=A, etc.)

Returns:

If function successful

AX	= sectors per cluster
BX	= number of available clusters
CX	= bytes per sector
DX	= clusters per drive

If function unsuccessful (drive invalid)

AX	= FFFFH

Notes:

■ This function regards "lost" clusters as being in use and does not report them as part of the number of available clusters, even though they are not assigned to a file.

■ Similar information is returned by Int 21H Functions 1BH and 1CH.

Int 21H Function 37H (55)   [2] [3]
Reserved

Int 21H Function 38H (56)   [2] [3]
Get or Set Country Information

[2] Obtains internationalization information for the current country.

[3] Obtains internationalization information for the current or specified country, or sets the current country code.

Call with:

If getting internationalization information

[2]

AH	= 38H	
AL	= 0	to get "current" country information
DS:DX	= segment:offset of buffer for returned information	

[3]

AH	= 38H	
AL	= 0	to get "current" country information
	1-FEH	to get information for countries with code < 255
	FFH	to get information for countries with code >= 255
BX	= country code, if AL = FFH	
DS:DX	= segment:offset of buffer for returned information	

If setting current country code (MS-DOS versions 3.0 and later)

AH	= 38H	
AL	= 1-0FEH	country code for countries with code < 255
	0FFH	for countries with code >= 255
BX	= country code, if AL = 0FFH	
DX	= FFFFH	

Returns:

If function successful
Carry flag   = clear

and, if getting internationalization information
BX   = country code
DS:DX   = segment:offset of buffer holding internationalization information

and buffer filled in as follows:
(for PC-DOS 2.0 and 2.1)

Byte(s)	Contents
00H-01H	date format
	0 = USA *m d y*
	1 = Europe *d m y*
	2 = Japan *y m d*
02H-03H	ASCIIZ currency symbol
04H-05H	ASCIIZ thousands separator
06H-07H	ASCIIZ decimal separator
08H-1FH	reserved

(for MS-DOS versions 2.0 and later, PC-DOS versions 3.0 and later)

Byte(s)	Contents
00H-01H	date format
	0 = USA *m d y*
	1 = Europe *d m y*
	2 = Japan *y m d*
02H-06H	ASCIIZ currency symbol string
07H-08H	ASCIIZ thousands separator character
09H-0AH	ASCIIZ decimal separator character
0BH-0CH	ASCIIZ date separator character
0DH-0EH	ASCIIZ time separator character
0FH	currency format
	bit 0 *= 0 if currency symbol precedes value*
	= 1 if currency symbol follows value
	bit 1 *= 0 if no space between value and currency symbol*
	= 1 if one space between value and currency symbol
10H	number of digits after decimal in currency
11H	time format
	bit 0 *= 0 if 12-hour clock*
	= 1 if 24-hour clock

12H-15H	case-map call address
16H-17H	ASCIIZ data-list separator
18H-21H	reserved

If function unsuccessful

| Carry flag | = set |
| AX | = error code |

Notes:

■ The default country code is determined by the KEYB*xx* keyboard driver file if one is loaded. Otherwise, the default country code is OEM dependent.

■ The previous contents of register CX may be destroyed by the Get Country Information subfunction.

■ The case-map call address is the segment:offset of a FAR procedure that performs country-specific mapping on character values from 80H through 0FFH. The procedure must be called with the character to be mapped in register AL. If an alternate value exists for that character, it is returned in AL; otherwise, AL is unchanged.

■ [3] The value in register DX is used by MS-DOS to select between the Set Country and Get Country Information subfunctions.

■ [3.3] Int 21H Function 65H (Get Extended Country Information) returns a superset of the internationalization information supplied by this function.

Int 21H Function 39H (57)   [2] [3]
Create Directory

Creates a directory using the specified drive and path.

Call with:

| AH | = 39H |
| DS:DX | = segment:offset of ASCIIZ pathname |

Returns:

If function successful

| Carry flag | = clear |

If function unsuccessful

| Carry flag | = set |
| AX | = error code |

Note:

■ The function fails if:
  – any element of the pathname does not exist.
  – a directory with the same name at the end of the same path already exists.
  – the parent directory for the new directory is the root directory and is full.
  – the program is running on a network and the user running the program has insufficient access rights.

Int 21H Function 3AH (58)   [2] [3]
Delete Directory

Removes a directory using the specified drive and path.

Call with:

AH   = 3AH
DS:DX   = segment:offset of ASCIIZ pathname

Returns:

If function successful
Carry flag = clear

If function unsuccessful
Carry flag = set
AX   = error code

Note:

■ The function fails if:
  – any element of the pathname does not exist.
  – the specified directory is also the current directory.
  – the specified directory contains any files.
  – [3] the program is running on a network and the user running the program has insufficient access rights.

Int 21H Function 3BH (59)   [2] [3]
Set Current Directory

Sets the current, or default, directory using the specified drive and path.

Call with:

AH   = 3BH
DS:DX   = segment:offset of ASCIIZ pathname

Returns:

If function successful
Carry flag = clear

If function unsuccessful
Carry flag = set
AX   = error code

Notes:

- The function fails if any element of the pathname does not exist.

- Int 21H Function 47H can be used to obtain the name of the current directory before using Int 21H Function 3BH to select another so that the original directory can be restored later.

Int 21H Function 3CH (60)   [2] [3]
Create File

Given an ASCIIZ pathname, creates a new file in the designated or default directory on the designated or default disk drive. If the specified file already exists, it is truncated to zero length. In either case, the file is opened and a handle is returned that can be used by the program for subsequent access to the file.

Call with:

AH   = 3CH
CX   = file attribute

       00H   *if normal*
       01H   *if read-only*
       02H   *if hidden*
       04H   *if system*
DS:DX   = segment:offset of ASCIIZ pathname

Returns:

If function successful
Carry flag = clear
AX   = handle

If function failed
Carry flag = set
AX   = error code

Notes:

- The function fails if:
  - any element of the pathname does not exist.
  - the file is being created in the root directory and the root directory is full.
  - a file with the same name and the read-only attribute already exists in the specified directory.
  - [3] the program is running on a network and the user running the program has insufficient access rights.

- If the volume label or directory bits are set in the file attribute passed in register CX, they are ignored by MS-DOS.

- A file is usually given a normal (00H) attribute when it is created. The file's attribute can subsequently be modified with Int 21H Function 43H.

- [3] See also Int 21H Function 5BH, which protects against the inadvertent destruction of existing file data, and Int 21H Function 5AH, which aids in the creation of temporary working files.

Int 21H Function 3DH (61)   [2] [3]
Open File

Given an ASCIIZ pathname, opens the specified file in the designated or default directory on the designated or default disk drive. A handle is returned that can be used by the program for subsequent access to the file.

Call with:

AH	= 3DH			
AL	= access mode			
[2]	*bits 3–7 =*	*00000*	*(reserved)*	
	bits 0–2 =	*000*	*if read access*	
		001	*if write access*	
		010	*if read/write access*	
[3]	*bit 7 =*	*inheritance flag*		
		0	*if handle inherited by child processes*	
		1	*if handle not inherited*	

bits 4–6 =	*sharing mode*	
	000	*if compatibility mode*
	001	*if deny all*
	010	*if deny write*
	011	*if deny read*
	100	*if deny none*
bit 3 =	*0*	*(reserved)*
bits 0–2 =	*000*	*if read access*
	001	*if write access*
	010	*if read/write access*

DS:DX = segment:offset of ASCIIZ pathname

Returns:

If function successful
Carry flag = clear
AX = handle

If function unsuccessful
Carry flag = set
AX = error code

Notes:

- Any normal, system, or hidden file with a matching name will be opened by this function. If the file is read-only, the success of the operation also depends on the access code in bits 0–2 of register AL. After opening the file, the file read/write pointer is set to offset zero (the first byte of the file).

- [2] Only bits 0–2 of register AL are significant; the remaining bits should be zero for upward compatibility.
  [3] Bit 3 should always be zero; bits 4–7 control access to the file by other programs. Bits 4–6 have no effect unless SHARE.EXE is loaded.

- The function fails if:
  – any element of the pathname does not exist.
  – the file is opened with an access mode of read/write and the file has the read-only attribute.
  – [3] SHARE.EXE is loaded and the file has already been opened by one or more other processes in a sharing mode that is incompatible with the current program's request.

- The file's date and time stamp can be accessed after a successful open call with Int 21H Function 57H.

- The file's attributes (hidden, system, read-only, or archive) can be obtained with Int 21H Function 43H.

- When a file handle is inherited by a child process or is duplicated with Int 21H Functions 45H or 46H, all sharing and access restrictions are also inherited.

- [3] A file-sharing error causes a critical-error exception (Int 24H) with an error code of 02H. Int 21H Function 59H can be used to obtain information about the sharing violation.

Int 21H Function 3EH (62)   [2] [3]
Close File

Given a handle that was obtained by a previous successful open (Int 21H Function 3DH) or create (Int 21H Function 3CH, 5AH, or 5BH) operation, flushes all internal buffers associated with the file to disk, closes the file, and releases the handle for reuse. If the file was modified, the time and date stamp and file size are updated in the file's directory entry.

Call with:

    AH   = 3EH
    BX   = handle

Returns:

If function successful
Carry flag = clear

If function unsuccessful
Carry flag = set
AX   = error code

Note:

- If you accidentally call this function with a zero handle, the standard input device is closed, and the keyboard appears to go dead. Be sure you always call the close function with a valid, non-zero handle.

Int 21H Function 3FH (63)   [2] [3]
Read File or Device

Given a valid file handle from a previous open (Int 21H Function 3DH) or create (Int 21H Function 3CH, 5AH, or 5BH) operation, a buffer address, and a length in bytes, transfers data at the current file pointer position from the file into the buffer and then updates the file pointer position.

Call with:

AH	= 3FH
BX	= handle
CX	= number of bytes to read
DS:DX	= segment:offset of buffer area

Returns:

If function successful
Carry flag = clear
AX = bytes transferred

If function unsuccessful
Carry flag = set
AX = error code

Notes:

- If reading from a character device (such as the standard input) in cooked mode, at most one line of input will be read (i.e., up to a carriage return character or the specified length, whichever comes first).

- If the carry flag is returned clear but AX = 0, then the file pointer was already at end of file when the program requested the read.

- If the carry flag is returned clear but AX < CX, then a partial record was read at end of file or there is an error.

- [3] If the program is running on a network, the user must have Read access rights to the directory and file.

Int 21H Function 40H (64) [2] [3]
Write File or Device

Given a valid file handle from a previous open (Int 21H Function 3DH) or create (Int 21H Function 3CH, 5AH, or 5BH) operation, a buffer address, and a length in bytes, transfers data from the buffer into the file and then updates the file pointer position.

Call with:

AH	= 40H
BX	= handle
CX	= number of bytes to write
DS:DX	= segment:offset of buffer area

Returns:

If function successful
Carry flag = clear
AX = bytes transferred

If function unsuccessful
Carry flag = set
AX = error code

Notes:

- If the carry flag is returned clear but AX < CX, then a partial record was written or there is an error. This can be caused by a Ctrl-Z (1AH) embedded in the data if the destination is a character device in cooked mode or by a disk-full condition if the destination is a file.

- If the function is called with CX = 0, the file is truncated or extended to the current file pointer position.

- [3] If the program is running on a network, the user must have Write access rights to the directory and file.

Int 21H Function 41H (65) [2] [3]
Delete File

Deletes a file from the specified or default disk and directory.

Call with:

AH	= 41H
DS:DX	= segment:offset of ASCIIZ pathname

Returns:

If function successful
Carry flag = clear

If function unsuccessful
Carry flag = set
AX = error code

Notes:

- This function deletes a file by replacing the first character of its filename in the directory with the character *e* (E5H) and marking the file's clusters as "free" in the disk's file allocation table. The actual data stored in those clusters is not overwritten.

- Only one file at a time may be deleted with this function. Unlike the FCB-related Delete File function (Int 21H Function 13H), the *∗* and *?* wildcard characters are not allowed in the file specification.

- The function fails if:
  - any element of the pathname does not exist.
  - the designated file exists but has the read-only attribute (Int 21H Function 43H can be used to examine and modify a file's attribute before attempting to delete it).
  - [3] the program is running on a network, and the user running the program has insufficient access rights.

Int 21H Function 42H (66) [2] [3]
Set File Pointer

Sets the file location pointer relative to the start of file, end of file, or current file position.

Call with:

AH	= 42H
AL	= method code
	00H absolute offset from start of file
	01H signed offset from current file pointer
	02H signed offset from end of file
BX	= handle
CX	= most significant half of offset
DX	= least significant half of offset

Returns:

If function successful

Carry flag	= clear
DX	= most significant half of resulting file pointer
AX	= least significant half of resulting file pointer

If function unsuccessful

Carry flag	= set
AX	= error code

Notes:

■ This function uses a method code and a double-precision (32-bit) value to set the file pointer. The next record read or written in the file will begin at the new file pointer location.

■ Method 02H may be used to find the size of the file by calling Int 21H Function 42H with an offset of 0 and examining the pointer location that is returned.

■ Using methods 01H or 02H, it is possible to set the file pointer to a location that is before the start of file. If this is done, no error is returned by this function, but an error will be encountered upon a subsequent attempt to read or write the file.

■ No matter what method is used in the call to this function, the file pointer returned in DX:AX is always the resulting absolute byte offset from the start of file.

Int 21H Function 43H (67) [2] [3]
Get or Set File Attributes

Obtains or alters the attributes of a file (read-only, hidden, system, or archive).

Call with:

AH	= 43H
AL	= 00H if getting file attribute
	01H if setting file attribute
CX	= new file attribute, if AL = 01
	bit 5 = *archive*
	bit 2 = *system*
	bit 1 = *hidden*
	bit 0 = *read-only*
DS:DX	= segment:offset of ASCIIZ pathname

Returns:

If function successful
Carry flag = clear
CX = file attribute (see above)

If function unsuccessful
Carry flag = set
AX = error code

Notes:

- Bit 0 of the attribute is the rightmost, or least significant, bit. Attribute bits may be combined; for example, an attribute value of 3 indicates a hidden, read-only file.

- This function cannot be used to set the volume label bit (bit 3) or directory bit (bit 4) on an existing file.

- [3] If the program is running on a network, the user must have Create access rights to the directory containing the file whose attribute is to be modified.

Int 21H Function 44H (68) [2] [3]
IOCTL (I/O Control)

Provides a direct path of communication between an application program and a device driver. Allows a program to obtain hardware-dependent information and to request operations that are not supported by other MS-DOS function calls.

The IOCTL subfunctions and the MS-DOS versions in which they first became available are:

Subfunction	Name	MS-DOS version
00H	Get Device Information	2.0
01H	Set Device Information	2.0
02H	Receive Control Data from Character Device Driver	2.0
03H	Send Control Data to Character Device Driver	2.0
04H	Receive Control Data from Block Device Driver	2.0
05H	Send Control Data to Block Device Driver	2.0
06H	Check Input Status	2.0
07H	Check Output Status	2.0
08H	Check If Block Device Is Removable	3.0
09H	Check If Block Device Is Remote	3.1
0AH	Check If Handle Is Remote	3.1
0BH	Change Sharing Retry Count	3.1

(continued)

Subfunction	Name	MS-DOS version
0CH	Generic I/O Control for Character Devices	
	CL = 45H: Set Iteration Count	3.2
	CL = 4AH: Select Code Page	3.3
	CL = 4CH: Start Code Page Preparation	3.3
	CL = 4DH: End Code Page Preparation	3.3
	CL = 65H: Get Iteration Count	3.2
	CL = 6AH: Query Selected Code Page	3.3
	CL = 6BH: Query Prepare List	3.3
0DH	Generic I/O Control for Block Devices	
	CL = 40H: Set Device Parameters	3.2
	CL = 41H: Write Track	3.2
	CL = 42H: Format and Verify Track	3.2
	CL = 60H: Get Device Parameters	3.2
	CL = 61H: Read Track	3.2
	CL = 62H: Verify Track	3.2
0EH	Get Logical Drive Map	3.2
0FH	Set Logical Drive Map	3.2

Only IOCTL Subfunctions 00H, 06H, and 07H may be used for handles associated with files. Subfunctions 00H–08H are not supported on network devices.

Int 21H Function 44H (68) [2]
Subfunction 00H
IOCTL: Get Device Information

Returns a device information word for the file or device associated with the specified handle.

Call with:

```
AH      = 44H
AL      = 00H
BX      = handle
```

Returns:

If function successful
Carry flag = clear
DX = device information word
        For a file:
        bits 8–15 = 0 (reserved)
        bit 7 = 0 indicating a file
        bit 6 = 0 file has been written
                1 file has not been written
        bits 0–5 = drive number (0=A, 1=B, etc.)
        For a device:
        bit 15 = reserved
        bit 14 = 1 if device supports IOCTL Read and
                Write Control Data subfunctions
                0 if Control Data subfunctions not
                supported
        bits 8–13 = reserved
        bit 7 = 1 indicating a device
        bit 6 = 0 if end of file on input
        bit 5 = 0 if handle in cooked mode
                1 if handle in raw mode
        bit 4 = reserved
        bit 3 = 1 if clock device
        bit 2 = 1 if NUL device
        bit 1 = 1 if standard output
        bit 0 = 1 if standard input

If function unsuccessful
Carry flag = set
AX = error code

Notes:

- Bits 8–15 of DX correspond to the upper 8 bits of the device driver attribute word.

- Bit 5 of the device information word for a handle associated with a character device signifies whether MS-DOS considers that handle to be in "raw mode" or "cooked mode." In cooked mode, MS-DOS filters the character stream and may take special action when the characters Ctrl-C, Ctrl-S, Ctrl-P, Ctrl-Z, and carriage return are detected. In raw mode, all characters are treated as data, and the exact number of characters requested is always read or written.

Int 21H Function 44H (68) [2]
Subfunction 01H
IOCTL: Set Device Information

Sets certain flags for a handle associated with a character device. This subfunction may not be used for a handle that is associated with a file.

Call with:

AH	= 44H
AL	= 01H
BX	= handle
DX	= device information word

    bits 8–15 = 0 (reserved)
    bit 7   = 1 indicating a device
    bit 6   = 0 (reserved)
    bit 5   = 0 to select cooked mode
                   1 to select raw mode
    bit 4   = 0 (reserved)
    bit 3   = 1 if clock device
    bit 2   = 1 if NUL device
    bit 1   = 1 if standard output
    bit 0   = 1 if standard input

Returns:

If function successful
Carry flag = clear

If function unsuccessful
Carry flag = set
AX   = error code

Notes:

- If register DH does not contain 00H, control returns to the program with the carry flag set and error code 0001H (invalid function) in register AX.

- Bit 5 of the information word for a handle associated with a character device signifies whether MS-DOS considers that handle to be in "raw mode" or "cooked mode." See Notes for IOCTL Subfunction 00H.

Int 21H Function 44H (68)   [2]
Subfunction 02H
IOCTL: Read Control Data from Character Device Driver

Reads control data from a character device driver. The length and contents of the data are specific to each device driver and do not follow any standard format. This function does not necessarily result in any input from the physical device.

Call with:

AH	= 44H
AL	= 02H
BX	= handle
CX	= number of bytes to read
DS:DX	= segment:offset of buffer to receive data

Returns:

If function successful
Carry flag = clear
AX = bytes read

and buffer contains control data from driver

If function unsuccessful
Carry flag = set
AX = error code

Notes:

■ If supported by the driver, this subfunction can be used to obtain hardware-dependent status and availability information that is not supported by other MS-DOS function calls.

■ Character device drivers are not required to support IOCTL Subfunction 02H. A program can test bit 14 of the device information word returned by IOCTL Subfunction 00H to determine whether the driver supports this subfunction. If Subfunction 02H is requested and the driver does not have the ability to process control data, control returns to the program with the carry flag set and error code 0001H (invalid function) in register AX.

Int 21H Function 44H (68) [2]
Subfunction 03H
IOCTL: Write Control Data to Character Device Driver

Transfers control data from an application to a character device driver. The length and contents of the data are specific to each device driver and do not follow any standard format. This function does not necessarily result in any output to the physical device.

Call with:

AH	= 44H
AL	= 03H
BX	= handle
CX	= number of bytes to write
DS:DX	= segment:offset of data

Returns:

If function successful
Carry flag = clear
AX = bytes transferred

If function unsuccessful
Carry flag = set
AX = error code

Notes:

- If supported by the driver, this subfunction can be used to request hardware-dependent operations (such as setting baud rate for a serial port) that are not supported by other MS-DOS function calls.

- Character device drivers are not required to support IOCTL Subfunction 03H. A program can test bit 14 of the device information word returned by IOCTL Subfunction 00H to determine whether the driver supports this subfunction. If Subfunction 03H is requested and the driver does not have the ability to process control data, control returns to the program with the carry flag set and error code 0001H (invalid function) in register AX.

Int 21H Function 44H (68) [2]
Subfunction 04H
IOCTL: Read Control Data from Block Device Driver

Transfers control data from a block device driver directly into an application program's buffer. The length and contents of the data are specific to each device driver and do not follow any standard format. This function does not necessarily result in any input from the physical device.

Call with:

AH	= 44H
AL	= 04H
BL	= drive code (0=default, 1=A, 2=B, etc.)
CX	= number of bytes to read
DS:DX	= segment:offset of buffer

Returns:

If function successful
Carry flag = clear
AX = bytes transferred

and buffer contains control data from device driver
If function unsuccessful
Carry flag = set
AX = error code

Notes:

■ When supported by the driver, this subfunction can be used to obtain hardware-dependent status and availability information that is not provided by other MS-DOS function calls.

■ Block device drivers are not required to support IOCTL Subfunction 04H. If this subfunction is requested and the driver does not have the ability to process control data, control returns to the program with the carry flag set and error code 0001H (invalid function) in register AX.

Int 21H Function 44H (68) [2]
Subfunction 05H
IOCTL: Write Control Data to Block Device Driver

Transfers control data from an application program directly to a block device driver. The length and contents of the control data are specific to each device driver and do not follow any standard format. This function does not necessarily result in any output to the physical device.

Call with:

AH	= 44H
AL	= 05H
BL	= drive code (0=default, 1=A, 2=B, etc.)
CX	= number of bytes to write
DS:DX	= segment:offset of data

Returns:

If function successful
Carry flag = clear
AX = bytes transferred

If function unsuccessful
Carry flag = set
AX = error code

Notes:

- When supported by the driver, this subfunction can be used to request hardware-dependent operations (such as tape rewind or disk eject) that are not provided by other MS-DOS function calls.

- Block device drivers are not required to support IOCTL Subfunction 05H. If this subfunction is requested and the driver does not have the ability to process control data, control returns to the program with the carry flag set and error code 0001H (invalid function) in register AX.

Int 21H Function 44H (68) [2]
Subfunction 06H
IOCTL: Check Input Status

Returns a code indicating whether the device or file associated with a handle is ready for input.

Call with:

AH	= 44H
AL	= 06H
BX	= handle

Returns:

If function successful
Carry flag = clear

and, for a device:

AL	= 00H	if device not ready
	FFH	if device ready

or, for a file:

AL	= 00H	if file pointer at EOF
	FFH	if file pointer not at EOF

If function unsuccessful
Carry flag = set
AX = error code

Note:

■ This function can be used to check the status of character devices, such as the serial port or printer, that do not have their own "traditional" MS-DOS status calls.

Int 21H Function 44H (68) [2]
Subfunction 07H
IOCTL: Check Output Status

Returns a code indicating whether the device associated with a handle is ready for output.

Call with:

AH	= 44H
AL	= 07H
BX	= handle

Returns:

If function successful
Carry flag = clear

and, for a device:
AL   = 00H   if device not ready
            FFH   if device ready

or, for a file:
AL   = FFH

If function unsuccessful
Carry flag = set
AX   = error code

Note:

- When used with a handle for a file, this function always returns a ready status, even if the disk is full or no disk is in the drive.

Int 21H Function 44H (68)   [3]
Subfunction 08H
IOCTL: Check If Block Device Is Removable

Checks whether the specified block device contains a removable storage medium, such as a floppy disk.

Call with:

AH	= 44H
AL	= 08H
BL	= drive number (0=default, 1=A, 2=B, etc.)

Returns:

If function successful
Carry flag = clear
AL   = 00H   if medium is removable
            01H   if medium is not removable

If function unsuccessful
Carry flag = set
AX   = error code

Notes:

■ If a file is not found as expected on a particular drive, a program can use this subfunction to determine whether the user should be prompted to insert another disk.

■ This subfunction may not be used for a network drive.

■ Block drivers are not required to support Subfunction 08H. If this subfunction is requested and the block device cannot supply the information, control returns to the program with the carry flag set and error code 0001H (invalid function) in register AX.

Int 21H Function 44H (68)   [3.1]
Subfunction 09H
IOCTL: Check If Block Device Is Remote

Checks whether the specified block device is local (attached to the computer running the program) or remote (redirected to a network server).

Call with:

AH	= 44H
AL	= 09H
BL	= drive number (0=default, 1=A, 2=B, etc.)

Returns:

If function successful
Carry flag = clear
DX = device attribute word
    bit 12 = 0 if drive is local
               1 if drive is remote

If function unsuccessful
Carry flag = set
AX = error code

Note:

■ Use of this subfunction should be avoided. Application programs should not distinguish between files on local and remote devices.

Int 21H Function 44H (68) [3.1]
Subfunction 0AH
IOCTL: Check If Handle Is Remote

Checks whether the specified handle refers to a file or device that is local (located on the PC that is running the program) or remote (located on a network server).

Call with:

AH	= 44H
AL	= 0AH
BX	= handle

Returns:

If function successful
Carry flag = clear
DX = attribute word for file or device
   bit 15 = 0 if local
        1 if remote

If function unsuccessful
Carry flag = set
AX = error code

Notes:

■ Application programs should not ordinarily attempt to distinguish between files on local and remote devices.

■ If the network has not been started, control returns to the calling program with the carry flag set and error code 0001H (invalid function) in register AX.

Int 21H Function 44H (68) [3.1]
Subfunction 0BH
IOCTL: Change Sharing Retry Count

Sets the number of times MS-DOS retries a disk operation after a failure caused by a file-sharing violation before it returns an error to the requesting process. This subfunction is not available unless the file-sharing module (SHARE.EXE) is loaded.

Call with:

AH	= 44H
AL	= 0BH
CX	= delays per retry (default=1)
DX	= number of retries (default=3)

Returns:

If function successful
Carry flag = clear

If function unsuccessful
Carry flag = set
AX = error code

Notes:

■ The length of a delay is a machine-dependent value determined by the CPU type and clock speed. Each delay consists of the following instruction sequence:

```
xor  cx,cx
loop $
```

which executes 65,536 times before falling out of the loop.

■ The sharing retry count affects the behavior of the system as a whole and is not a local parameter for the process. If a program changes the sharing retry count, it should restore the default values before terminating.

Int 21H Function 44H (68) [3.2]
Subfunction 0CH
IOCTL: Generic I/O Control for Character Devices

Provides a general-purpose mechanism for communication between application programs and character device drivers.

Call with:

AH	= 44H
AL	= 0CH

BX	= handle
CH	= category (major) code:

00 = *unknown*

01 = *COM1, COM2, COM3, or COM4 (3.3)*

03 = *CON (keyboard and display) (3.3)*

05 = *LPT1, LPT2, or LPT3 (3.2)*

CL = function (minor) code:

45H = *Set Iteration Count (3.2)*

4AH = *Select Code Page (3.3)*

4CH = *Start Code Page Preparation (3.3)*

4DH = *End Code Page Preparation (3.3)*

65H = *Get Iteration Count (3.2)*

6AH = *Query Selected Code Page (3.3)*

6BH = *Query Prepare List (3.3)*

DS:DX = segment:offset of parameter block

Returns:

If function successful
Carry flag = clear

and, if called with CL = 65H, 6AH, or 6BH
DS:DX = segment:offset of parameter block

If function unsuccessful
Carry flag = set
AX = error code

Notes:

■ If the minor code is 45H (Set Iteration Count) or 65H (Get Iteration Count), the parameter block is simply a 2-byte buffer containing or receiving the iteration count for the printer. This call is valid only for printer drivers that support *Output Until Busy*, and determines the number of times the device driver will wait for the device to signal *ready* before returning from the output call.

■ The parameter block for minor codes 4AH (Select Code Page), 4DH (End Code Page Preparation), or 6AH (Query Code Page) has the following format:

```
dw      2               ; length of following data
dw      ?               ; code page ID
```

- The parameter block for minor code 4CH (Start Code Page Preparation) has the following format:

```
dw      0               ; flags
dw      (n+1)*2         ; length of remainder of
                        ;   parameter block
dw      n               ; number of code pages in
                        ;   the following list
dw      ?               ; code page 1
dw      ?               ; code page 2
.
.
.
dw      ?               ; code page n
```

- The parameter block for minor code 6BH (Query Prepare List) has the following format, assuming *n* hardware code pages and *m* prepared code pages ($n <= 12$, $m <= 12$):

```
dw      (n+m+2)*2       ; length of following data
dw      n               ; no. of hardware code pages
dw      ?               ; hardware code page 1
dw      ?               ; hardware code page 2
.
.
.
dw      ?               ; hardware code page n
dw      m               ; no. of prepared code pages
dw      ?               ; prepared code page 1
dw      ?               ; prepared code page 2
.
.
.
dw      ?               ; prepared code page m
```

- After a minor code 4CH (Start Code Page Preparation) call, the data defining the code page font is written to the driver using one or more calls to the IOCTL Write Control Data subfunction (Interrupt 21H, Function 44H, Subfunction 03H). The format of the data is device- and driver-specific. After the font data has been written to the driver, a minor code 4DH (End Code Page Preparation) call must be issued. If no data is written to the driver between the minor code 4CH and 4DH calls, the driver interprets the newly prepared code pages as hardware code pages.

- A special variation of the minor code 4CH (Start Code Page Preparation) call, called ''Refresh,'' is required to actually load the peripheral device with the prepared code pages. The refresh operation is obtained by requesting minor code 4CH with each code page position in the parameter block set to −1, followed by an immediate call for minor code 4DH (End Code Page Preparation).

Int 21H Function 44H [3.2]
Subfunction 0DH
IOCTL: Generic I/O Control for Block Devices

Provides a general-purpose mechanism for communication between application programs and block device drivers. Allows a program to inspect or change device parameters for a logical drive and to read, write, format, and verify disk tracks in a hardware-independent manner.

Call with:

AH	= 44H
AL	= 0DH
BL	= drive code (0=default, 1=A, 2=B, etc.)
CH	= category (major) code:
	08H = *disk drive*
CL	= function (minor) code:
	40H = *Set Device Parameters*
	41H = *Write Track*
	42H = *Format and Verify Track*
	60H = *Get Device Parameters*
	61H = *Read Track*
	62H = *Verify Track*
DS:DX	= segment:offset of parameter block

Returns:

If function successful
Carry flag = clear

and, if called with CL = 60H or 61H
DS:DX = segment:offset of parameter block

If function unsuccessful
Carry flag = set
AX = error code

Notes:

■ The minor code 40H (Set Device Parameters) function must be used before an attempt to write, read, format, or verify a track on a logical drive. In general, the following sequence applies to any of these operations:

– Get the current parameters (minor code 60H). Examine and save them.
– Set the new parameters (minor code 40H).
– Perform the task.
– Retrieve the original parameters and restore them with minor code 40H.

■ For minor codes 40H (Set Device Parameters) and 60H (Get Device Parameters), the parameter block is formatted as follows:

Special-functions field: offset 00H, length = 1 byte

Bit(s)	Value	Meaning
0	0	Device BPB field contains a new default BPB
	1	Use current BPB
1	0	Use all fields in parameter block
	1	Use track layout field only
2	0	Sectors in track may be different sizes (should always be avoided)
	1	Sectors in track are all same size; sector numbers range from 1 to the total number of sectors in the track (should always be used)
3–7	0	Reserved

Device type field: offset 01H, length 1 byte

Value	Meaning
0	320/360 KB, 5.25-inch disk
1	1.2 MB, 5.25-inch disk
2	720 KB, 3.5-inch disk
3	Single-density, 8-inch disk
4	Double-density, 8-inch disk
5	Fixed disk
6	Tape drive
7	Other type of block device

Device attributes field: offset 02H, length 1 word

Bit(s)	Value	Meaning
0	0	Removable storage medium
	1	Nonremovable storage medium
1	0	Door lock not supported
	1	Door lock supported
2–15	0	Reserved

Number of cylinders field: offset 04H, length 1 word

Maximum number of cylinders supported on the block device

Media type field: offset 06H, length 1 byte

Value	Meaning
0	1.2 MB, 5.25-inch disk
1	320/360 KB, 5.25-inch disk

Device BPB field: offset 07H, length 31 bytes

For format of the device BPB, see separate Note below.

If bit 0 = 0 in special-functions field, this field contains the new default BPB for the device.

If bit 0 = 1 in special-functions field, the BPB in this field is returned by the device driver in response to subsequent Build BPB requests.

Track layout field: offset 26H, variable-length table

Length	Meaning
Word	Number of sectors in track
Word	Number of first sector in track
Word	Size of first sector in track
.	
.	
.	
Word	Number of last sector in track
Word	Size of last sector in track

■ The device BPB field is a 31-byte data structure that describes the current disk and its control areas. The field is formatted as follows:

Byte(s)	Meaning
00H–01H	Bytes per sector
02H	Sectors per cluster (allocation unit)

Byte(s)	Meaning
03H–04H	Reserved sectors, beginning at sector 0
05H	Number of file allocation tables (FATs)
06H–07H	Maximum number of root-directory entries
08H–09H	Number of sectors
0AH	Media descriptor
0BH–0CH	Sectors per FAT
0DH–0EH	Sectors per track
0FH–10H	Number of heads
11H–14H	Number of hidden sectors
15H–1FH	Reserved

■ When minor code 40H (Set Device Parameters) is used, the number of cylinders should not be altered, or some or all of the volume may become inaccessible.

■ For minor codes 41H (Write Track) and 61H (Read Track), the parameter block is formatted as follows:

Byte(s)	Meaning
00H	Special-functions field (must be 0)
01H–02H	Head
03H–04H	Cylinder
05H–06H	Starting sector
07H–08H	Sectors to transfer
09H–0CH	Transfer buffer address

■ For minor codes 42H (Format and Verify Track) and 62H (Verify Track), the parameter block is formatted as follows:

Byte(s)	Meaning
00H	Special-functions field (must be 0)
01H–02H	Head
03H–04H	Cylinder

Int 21H Function 44H (68)   [3.2]
Subfunction 0EH
IOCTL: Get Logical Drive Map

Returns the logical drive code that was most recently used to access the specified block device.

Call with:

AH   = 44H
AL   = 0EH
BL   = drive code (0=default, 1=A, 2=B, etc.)

Returns:

If function successful
Carry flag = clear
AL   = mapping code

     00H   *if only one logical drive code assigned to the block device*

     01H–1AH   *logical drive code (1=A, 2=B, etc.) mapped to the block device*

If function unsuccessful
Carry flag = set
AX   = error code

Note:

- If a drive has not been assigned a logical mapping with Function 44H Subfunction 0FH, the logical and physical drive codes are the same.

Int 21H Function 44H (68)   [3.2]
Subfunction 0FH
IOCTL: Set Logical Drive Map

Sets the next logical drive code that will be used to reference a block device.

Call with:

AH   = 44H
AL   = 0FH
BL   = drive code (0=default, 1=A, 2=B, etc.)

Returns:

If function successful
Carry flag = clear

AL   = mapping code

> 00H   *if only one logical drive code*
>   *assigned to the block device*
> 01H–1AH   *logical drive code (1=A, 2=B, etc.)*
>   *mapped to the block device*

If function unsuccessful
Carry flag = set
AX   = error code

Note:

- When a physical block device is aliased to more than one logical drive code, this function can be used to inform the driver which drive code will next be used to access the device.

Int 21H Function 45H (69) [2] [3]
Duplicate Handle

Given a handle for a currently open device or file, returns a new handle that refers to the same device or file at the same position.

Call with:

AH   = 45H
BX   = handle to be duplicated

Returns:

If function successful
Carry flag = clear
AX   = new handle

If function unsuccessful
Carry flag = set
AX   = error code

Notes:

- A seek, read, or write operation that moves the file pointer for one of the two handles also moves the file pointer associated with the other.

- This function can be used to efficiently update the directory for a file that has changed in length, without incurring the overhead of closing and then reopening the file. The handle for the file is simply duplicated with this function and the duplicate is closed, leaving the original handle open for further read/write operations.

■ [3.3] See also Int 21H Function 68H (Commit File).

Int 21H Function 46H (70)   [2] [3]
Redirect Handle

Given two handles, makes the second handle refer to the same device
or file at the same location as the first handle. The second handle is
then said to be redirected.

Call with:

AH	= 46H
BX	= handle for file or device
CX	= handle to be redirected

Returns:

If function successful
Carry flag = clear

If function unsuccessful
Carry flag = set
AX = error code

Notes:

■ If the handle passed in CX already refers to an open file, that file is
closed first.

■ A seek, read, or write operation that moves the file pointer for one
of the two handles also moves the file pointer associated with the
other.

■ This function is commonly used to redirect the standard input and
output handles to another file or device before a child process is executed with Int 21H Function 4BH.

Int 21H Function 47H (71)   [2] [3]
Get Current Directory

Obtains an ASCIIZ string that describes the path from the root to the
current directory, and the name of that directory.

Call with:

AH   = 47H
DL   = drive code (0=default,1=A, etc.)
DS:SI   = segment:offset of 64-byte buffer

Returns:

If function successful
Carry flag = clear

and buffer is filled in with full pathname from root of current directory

If function unsuccessful
Carry flag = set
AX   = error code

Notes:

- The returned path name does not include the drive identifier or a leading backslash (\). It is terminated with a null (00H) byte. Consequently, if the current directory is the root directory, the first byte in the buffer will contain 00H.

- The function fails if the drive code is invalid.

- The current directory may be set with Int 21H Function 3BH.

Int 21H Function 48H (72)   [2] [3]
Allocate Memory Block

Allocates a block of memory and returns a pointer to the beginning of the allocated area.

Call with:

AH   = 48H
BX   = number of paragraphs of memory needed

Returns:

If function successful
Carry flag = clear
AX   = initial segment of allocated block

If function unsuccessful
Carry flag = set
AX   = error code
BX   = size of largest available block (paragraphs)

Notes:

- If the function succeeds, the base address of the newly allocated block is AX:0000.

- The default allocation strategy used by MS-DOS is "first fit"; that is, the memory block at the lowest address that is large enough to satisfy the request is allocated. The allocation strategy can be altered with Int 21H Function 58H.

- When a .COM program is loaded, it ordinarily already "owns" all of the memory in the transient program area, leaving none for dynamic allocation. The amount of memory initially allocated to a .EXE program at load time depends on the MINALLOC and MAXALLOC fields in the .EXE file header. See Int 21H Function 4AH.

Int 21H Function 49H (73)   [2] [3]
Release Memory Block

Releases a memory block and makes it available for use by other programs.

Call with:

AH	= 49H
ES	= segment of block to be released

Returns:

If function successful
Carry flag = clear

If function unsuccessful
Carry flag = set
AX = error code

Notes:

- This function assumes that the memory block being released was previously obtained by a successful call to Int 21H Function 48H.

- The function will fail or can cause unpredictable system errors if:
  - the program releases a memory block that does not belong to it.
  - the segment address passed in register ES is not a valid base address for an existing memory block.

Int 21H Function 4AH (74)   [2] [3]
Resize Memory Block

Dynamically shrinks or extends a memory block, according to the needs of an application program.

Call with:

AH	= 4AH
BX	= desired new block size in paragraphs
ES	= segment of block to be modified

Returns:

If function successful
Carry flag = clear

If function unsuccessful
Carry flag = set
AX = error code
BX = maximum block size available (paragraphs)

Notes:

- This function modifies the size of a memory block that was previously allocated with a call to Int 21H Function 48H.

- If the program is requesting an increase in the size of an allocated block, and this function fails, the maximum possible size for the specified block is returned in register BX. The program can use this value to determine whether it should terminate, or continue in a degraded fashion with less memory.

- A program that uses EXEC (Int 21H Function 4BH) to load and execute a child program must call this function first, passing the address of its own PSP in register ES and the amount of memory needed for its own code, data, and stacks in register BX.

Int 21H Function 4BH (75)   [2] [3]
Execute Program (EXEC)

Allows an application program to run another program, regaining control when it is finished. Can also be used to load overlays although this use is uncommon.

Call with:

AH = 4BH
AL = subfunction
　　　00H = Load and Execute Program
　　　03H = Load Overlay
ES:BX = segment:offset of parameter block
DS:DX = segment:offset of program specification

Returns:

If function successful
Carry flag = clear

[2] all registers except for CS:IP may be destroyed
[3] registers are preserved in the usual fashion

If function unsuccessful
Carry flag = set
AX = error code

Notes:

- The parameter block format for Subfunction 00H (Load and Execute Program) is as follows:

Bytes	Contents
00H–01H	Segment pointer to environment block
02H–03H	Offset of command line tail
04H–05H	Segment of command line tail
06H–07H	Offset of first FCB to be copied into new PSP + 5CH
08H–09H	Segment of first FCB
0AH–0BH	Offset of second FCB to be copied into new PSP + 6CH
0CH–0DH	Segment of second FCB

- The parameter block format for Subfunction 03H (Load Overlay) is as follows:

Bytes	Contents
00H–01H	Segment address where overlay is to be loaded
02H–03H	Relocation factor to apply to loaded image

- The environment block must be paragraph aligned. It consists of a sequence of ASCIIZ strings in the form:

```
db    'COMSPEC=A:\COMMAND.COM',0
```

The entire set of strings is terminated by an extra null (00H) byte.

- The command tail format consists of a count byte, followed by an ASCII string, terminated by a carriage return (which is not included in the count). The first character in the string should be an ASCII space (20H) for compatibility with the command tail passed to programs by COMMAND.COM. For example:

```
db    6,' *.DAT',0dh
```

- Before a program uses Int 21H Function 4BH to run another program, it must release all memory it is not actually using with a call to Int 21H Function 4AH, passing the segment address of its own PSP and the number of paragraphs to retain.

- All active handles (open files and standard devices) of the parent program are inherited by the child program. If the parent redirects standard input and/or output to other devices or files, the child will inherit the same environment and will read its input from the redirected source.

- The environment block can be used to pass information to the child process. If the environment block pointer in the parameter block is zero, the child program inherits an exact copy of the parent's environment. In any case, the segment address of the child's environment is found at offset 002CH in the child's PSP.

- After return from the EXEC function call, the termination type and return code of the child program may be obtained with Int 21H Function 4DH.

Int 21H Function 4CH (76) [2] [3]
Terminate Process with Return Code

Terminates the current process, passing a return code to the parent process. This is one of several methods that a program can use to perform a final exit. MS-DOS then takes the following actions:

- All memory belonging to the process is released.
- File buffers are flushed and any open handles for files or devices owned by the process are closed.
- The termination handler vector (Int 22H) is restored from PSP:000AH.
- The Ctrl-C handler vector (Int 23H) is restored from PSP:000EH.

- [2] [3] The critical-error handler vector (Int 24H) is restored from PSP:0012H.

- Control is transferred to the termination handler.

If the program is returning to COMMAND.COM, control transfers to the resident portion and the transient portion is reloaded if necessary. If a batch file is in progress, the next line of the file is fetched and interpreted; otherwise, a prompt is issued for the next user command.

Call with:

AH = 4CH
AL = return code

Returns:

Nothing

Notes:

- [2] [3] This is the preferred method of termination for application programs, since it allows a return code to be passed to the parent program and does not rely on the contents of any segment register. Other methods of performing a final exit are:
  – Int 20H
  – Int 21H Function 00H
  – Int 21H Function 31H
  – Int 27H

- Any files that have been opened using FCBs and modified by the program should be closed before program termination; otherwise, data may be lost.

- The return code can be retrieved by the parent process with Int 21H Function 4DH (Get Return Code). It can also be tested in a batch file with an IF ERRORLEVEL statement. By convention, a return code of zero indicates successful execution, and a non-zero return code indicates an error.

- [3] If the program is running on a network, it should remove all locks it has placed on file regions before terminating.

Int 21H Function 4DH (77)   [2] [3]
Get Return Code

Used by a parent process, after the successful execution of an EXEC call (Int 21H Function 4BH), to obtain the return code and termination type of a child process.

Call with:

AH   = 4DH

Returns:

AH   = exit type
              00H if normal termination by Int 20H, Int 21H
                    Function 0, or Int 21H Function 4CH
              01H if termination by user's entry of CtrlDC
              02H if termination by critical-error handler
              03H if termination by Int 21H Function 31H or
                    Int 27H
AL   = return code passed by child process (0 if child termi-
              nated by Int 20H, Int 21H Function 0, or Int 27H)

Notes:

- This function will yield the return code of a child process only
  once. A subsequent call without an intervening EXEC (Int 21H
  Function 4BH) will not necessarily return any valid information.

- This function does not set the carry flag to indicate an error. If no
  previous child process has been executed, the values returned in
  AL and AH are undefined.

Int 21H Function 4EH (78)   [2] [3]
Find First File

Given a file specification in the form of an ASCIIZ string, searches
the default or specified directory on the default or specified drive for
the first matching file.

Call with:

AH   = 4EH
CX   = attribute to use in search
DS:DX   = segment:offset of ASCIIZ pathname

Returns:

If function successful (matching file found)
Carry flag   = clear

and current disk transfer area filled in as follows:

> bytes 0–20 = reserved
> byte 21   = attribute of matched file
> bytes 22–23 = file time
>> bits 0BH–0FH = hours (0–23)
>> bits 05H–0AH = minutes (0–59)
>> bits 00H–04H = 2-second increments (0–29)
> bytes 24–25 = file date
>> bits 09H–0FH = year (relative to 1980)
>> bits 05H–08H = month (1–12)
>> bits 00H–04H = day (1–31)
> bytes 26–29 = file size
> bytes 30–42 = ASCIIZ filename and extension

If function unsuccessful (no matching files)
Carry flag = set
AX   = error code

Notes:

- This function assumes that the DTA has been previously set by the program with Int 21H Function 1AH to point to a buffer of adequate size.

- The * and ? wildcard characters are allowed in the filename. If wildcard characters are present, this function returns only the first matching filename.

- If the attribute is 00H, only ordinary files are found. If the volume label attribute bit is set, only volume labels will be returned (if any are present). Any other attribute or combination of attributes (hidden, system, and directory) results in those files *and* all normal files being matched.

Int 21H Function 4FH (79)   [2] [3]
Find Next File

Assuming a previous successful call to Int 21H Function 4EH, finds the next file in the default or specified directory on the default or specified drive that matches the original file specification.

Call with:

AH   = 4FH

Assumes DTA points to working buffer used by previous successful Int 21H Function 4EH or 4FH.

Returns:

If function successful (matching file found)
Carry flag = clear

and current disk transfer area filled in as follows:
    bytes 0–20 = reserved
    byte 21   = attribute of matched file
    bytes 22–23 = file time
                bits 0BH–0FH = hours (0–23)
                bits 05H–0AH = minutes (0–59)
                bits 00H–04H = 2-second increments (0–29)
    bytes 24–25 = file date
                bits 09H–0FH = year (relative to 1980)
                bits 05H–08H = month (1–12)
                bits 00H–04H = day (1–31)
    bytes 26–29 = file size
    bytes 30–42 = ASCIIZ filename and extension

If function unsuccessful (no more matching files)
Carry flag = set
AX   = error code

Notes:

- Use of this call assumes that the original file specification passed to Int 21H Function 4EH contained one or more * or ? wildcard characters.

- When this function is called, the current disk transfer area (DTA) must contain information from a previous successful call to Int 21H Function 4EH or 4FH.

Int 21H Function 50H (80)   [2] [3]
Reserved

Int 21H Function 51H (81)   [2] [3]
Reserved

Int 21H Function 52H (82)   [2] [3]
Reserved

Int 21H Function 53H (83) [2] [3]
Reserved

Int 21H Function 54H (84) [2] [3]
Get Verify Flag

Obtains the current value of the system verify (read-after-write) flag.

Call with:

AH = 54H

Returns:

AL = current verify flag value
00H   if verify off
01H   if verify on

Notes:

■ Because read-after-write verification slows disk operations, the default state of the system verify flag is OFF.

■ The state of the system verify flag can be changed through a call to Int 21H Function 2EH or by the MS-DOS commands VERIFY ON and VERIFY OFF.

Int 21H Function 55H (85) [2] [3]
Reserved

Int 21H Function 56H (86) [2] [3]
Rename File

Renames a file and/or moves its directory entry to a different directory on the same disk.

Call with:

AH = 56H
DS:DX = segment:offset of current ASCIIZ pathname
ES:DI = segment:offset of new ASCIIZ pathname

Returns:

If function successful
Carry flag = clear

If function unsuccessful
Carry flag = set
AX = error code

Notes:

- The function fails if:
  - any element of the pathname does not exist.
  - a file with the new pathname already exists.
  - the current pathname specification contains a different disk drive than does the new pathname.
  - the file is being moved to the root directory and the root directory is full.
  - the program is running on a network and the user has insufficient access rights to either the existing file or the new directory.

- The * and ? wildcard characters are not allowed in either the current or new pathname specifications.

Int 21H Function 57H (87) [2] [3]
Get or Set File Date and Time

Obtains or modifies the date and time stamp in a file's directory entry.

Call with:

If getting date and time
AH = 57H
AL = 00H
BX = handle

If setting date and time

AH = 57H
AL = 01H
BX = handle
CX = time

bits 0BH–0FH	= *hours (0–23)*
bits 05H–0AH	= *minutes (0–59)*
bits 00H–04H	= *2-second increments (0–29)*

DX = date

bits 09H–0FH	= *year (relative to 1980)*
bits 05H–08H	= *month (1–12)*
bits 00H–04H	= *day (1–31)*

Returns:

If function successful
Carry flag = clear

and, if called with AL = 00H
CX = time
DX = date

If function unsuccessful
Carry flag = set
AX = error code

Notes:

- The file must have been previously opened or created via a successful call to Int 21H Function 3CH, 3DH, 5AH, or 5BH.

- The date and time are in the format used in the directory, with bit 0 the rightmost, or least significant, bit.

- If the 16-bit date for a file is set to zero, that file's date and time are not displayed on directory listings.

- A date and time set with this function will prevail, even if the file is modified afterwards before the handle is closed.

Int 21H Function 58H (88)   [3]
Get or Set Allocation Strategy

Obtains or changes the code indicating the current MS-DOS strategy for allocating memory blocks.

Call with:

If getting strategy code
AH   = 58H
AL   = 00H

If setting strategy code
AH   = 58H
AL   = 01H
BX   = desired strategy code
        00H = *first fit*
        01H = *best fit*
        02H = *last fit*

Returns:

If function successful
Carry flag = clear

and, if called with AL = 00H
AX   = current strategy code

If function unsuccessful
Carry flag = set
AX   = error code

Notes:

- The memory allocation strategies are:
  First Fit: MS-DOS searches the available memory blocks from low addresses to high addresses, assigning the first one large enough to satisfy the block allocation request.
  Best Fit: MS-DOS searches all available memory blocks and assigns the smallest available block that will satisfy the request, regardless of its position.
  Last Fit: MS-DOS searches the available memory blocks from high addresses to low addresses, assigning the highest one large enough to satisfy the block allocation request.

- The default MS-DOS memory allocation strategy is First Fit (code 0).

Int 21H Function 59H (89)   [3]
Get Extended Error Information

Obtains detailed error information after a previous unsuccessful Int 21H function call, including the recommended remedial action.

Call with:

AH	= 59H
BX	= 00

Returns:

AH   = 59H

AX	= extended error code

See table "MS-DOS Extended Error Codes," page 6

BH	= error class	
	01H	if out of resource (such as storage or handles)
	02H	if not error, but temporary situation (such as locked region in file) that can be expected to end
	03H	if authorization problem
	04H	if internal error in system software
	05H	if hardware failure
	06H	if system software failure not the fault of the active process (such as missing configuration files)
	07H	if application program error
	08H	if file or item not found
	09H	if file or item of invalid type or format
	0AH (10)	if file or item interlocked
	0BH (11)	if wrong disk in drive, bad spot on disk, or storage medium problem
	0CH (12)	if other error
BL	= recommended action	
	01H	retry reasonable number of times, then prompt user to select abort or ignore
	02H	retry reasonable number of times with delay between retries, then prompt user to select abort or ignore
	03H	get corrected information from user (typically caused by incorrect filename or drive specification)
	04H	abort application with cleanup (i.e., terminate the program in as orderly a manner as possible, releasing locks, closing files, etc.)
	05H	perform immediate exit without cleanup
	06H	ignore error
	07H	retry after user intervention to remove cause of error

CH   = error locus
            01H   *unknown*
            02H   *block device (disk or disk emulator)*
            03H   *network*
            04H   *serial device*
            05H   *memory*

[3]
ES:DI   = ASCIIZ volume label of disk to insert, if AX =
            0022H (invalid disk change)

Notes:

- This function may be called after any other Int 21H function call
  that returned an error status, in order to obtain more detailed information about the error type and the recommended action. If the
  previous Int 21H function call had no error, 0000H is returned in
  register AX. This function may also be called during the execution
  of a critical-error (Int 24H) handler.

- The contents of registers CL, DX, SI, DI, BP, DS, and ES are
  destroyed by this function.

- Note that extended error codes 13H–1FH (19–31) and 22H (34)
  correspond exactly to the error codes 0–0CH (0–12) and 0FH (15)
  returned by Int 24H.

- Microsoft documentation explicitly warns that new error codes will
  be added in future versions of MS-DOS, and you should not code
  your programs to recognize only specific error numbers if you
  want to ensure upward compatibility.

Int 21H Function 5AH (90)   [3]
Create Temporary File

Creates a file with a unique name, in the current or specified directory
on the default or specified disk drive, and returns a handle that can be
used by the program for subsequent access to the file. The name gener-
ated for the file is also returned in a buffer specified by the program.

Call with:

AH   = 5AH

CX	= attribute
	00H *if normal*
	01H *if read-only*
	02H *if hidden*
	04H *if system*
DS:DX	= segment:offset of ASCIIZ path

Returns:

If function successful

Carry flag	= clear
AX	= handle
DS:DX	= segment:offset of complete ASCIIZ pathname

If function unsuccessful

| Carry flag | = set |
| AX | = error code |

Notes:

- The ASCIIZ path supplied to this function should be followed by at least 13 additional bytes of buffer space. MS-DOS adds a backslash (\) to the supplied path, if necessary, then appends a null-terminated filename that is a function of the current time.

- Files created with this function are not automatically deleted when the calling program terminates.

- The function fails if
  - any element of the pathname does not exist.
  - the file is being created in the root directory and the root directory is full.

- [3] If the program is running on a network, the file is created and opened for read/write access in compatibility sharing mode.

- See also Int 21H Functions 3CH and 5BH, which provide additional facilities for creating files.

Int 21H Function 5BH (91)   [3]
Create New File

Given an ASCIIZ pathname, creates a file in the designated or default directory on the designated or default drive and returns a handle that can be used by the program for subsequent access to the file. If a file with the same name already exists, the function fails.

Call with:

AH   = 5BH
CX   = attribute

           00H   *if normal*
           01H   *if read-only*
           02H   *if hidden*
           04H   *if system*

DS:DX = segment:offset of ASCIIZ pathname

Returns:

If function successful
Carry flag = clear
AX   = handle

If function unsuccessful
Carry flag = set
AX   = error code

Notes:

■ The function fails if:
  – any element of the specified path does not exist.
  – a file with the identical pathname (i.e., the same filename and extension in the same location in the directory structure) already exists.
  – the file is being created in the root directory and the root directory is full.
  – [3] the program is running on a network and the user has insufficient access rights to the directory that will contain the file.

■ The file is usually given the *normal* attribute when it is created, and is opened for both read and write operations. The attribute can subsequently be modified with Int 21H Function 43H.

■ See also Int 21H Function 3CH. The two calls are identical, except that Function 5BH fails if a file with the same name already exists, rather than truncating the file to zero length. Int 21H Function 5AH provides an alternative means of creating temporary working files.

■ This function may be used to implement semaphores in a network or multitasking environment. If the function succeeds, the program has acquired the semaphore. To release the semaphore, the program simply deletes the file.

Int 21H Function 5CH (92)   [3]
Lock or Unlock File Region

Locks or unlocks a specified region of a file that was previously opened or created with Int 21H Functions 3CH, 3DH, 5AH, or 5BH. This function is not available unless the file-sharing module (SHARE.EXE) is loaded.

Call with:

AH	= 5CH	
AL	= 00H	if locking region
	01H	if unlocking region
BX	= handle	
CX	= high part of region offset	
DX	= low part of region offset	
SI	= high part of region length	
DI	= low part of region length	

Returns:

If function successful
Carry flag = clear

If function unsuccessful
Carry flag = set
AX = error code

Notes:

- This function is useful for file and record synchronization in a multitasking environment or network. Access to the file as a whole is controlled by the attribute and file-sharing parameters passed in open or create calls, and by the file's attributes, which are stored in its directory entry.

- The beginning location in the file to be locked or unlocked is supplied as a positive double precision integer, which is a byte offset into the file. The length of the region to be locked or unlocked is similarly supplied as a positive double precision integer.

- For every call to lock a region of a file, there must be a subsequent unlock call with exactly the same file offset and length.

- Locking beyond the current end of file is not an error.

- If a process terminates without releasing active locks on a file, the result is undefined.

- Programs that are loaded with the EXEC call (Int 21H Function 4BH) inherit the handles of their parent but not any active locks.

- Duplicate handles created with Int 21H Function 45H, or handles redirected to the file with Int 21H Function 46H, are allowed access to locked regions within the same process.

Int 21H Function 5DH (93) [3]
Reserved

Int 21H Function 5EH (94) [3.1]
Subfunction 00H
Get Machine Name

Returns the address of an ASCIIZ (null-terminated) string identifying the local computer. This function call is only available when Microsoft Networks is running.

Call with:

```
AH      = 5EH
AL      = 00H
DS:DX   = segment:offset of buffer to receive string
```

Returns:

If function successful
```
Carry flag  = clear
CH          = 00H       if name not defined
            <> 00H      if name defined
CL          = netBIOS name number (if CH<>0)
DX:DX       = segment:offset of identifier (if CH<>0)
```

If function unsuccessful
```
Carry flag  = set
AX          = error code
```

Notes:

- The computer identifier is a 15-byte string, padded with spaces and terminated with a null (00H) byte.

- The effect of this call is unpredictable if the file-sharing support module is not loaded.

Int 21H Function 5EH (94) [3.1]
Subfunction 02H
Set Printer Setup String

Specifies a string to be sent in front of all files directed to a particular
network printer, allowing users at different network nodes to specify
individualized operating modes on the same printer. This function call
is only available when Microsoft Networks is running.

Call with:

AH	= 5EH
AL	= 02H
BX	= redirection list index
CX	= length of setup string
DS:SI	= segment:offset of setup string

Returns:

If function successful
Carry flag = clear

If function unsuccessful
Carry flag = set
AX = error code

Notes:

■ The redirection list index passed in register BX is obtained with
Function 5FH Subfunction 02H (Get Redirection List Entry).

■ See also Function 5EH Subfunction 03H, which may be used to obtain the existing setup string for a particular network printer.

Int 21H Function 5EH (94) [3.1]
Subfunction 03H
Get Printer Setup String

Obtains the printer setup string for a particular network printer. This
function call is only available when Microsoft Networks is running.

Call with:

AH   = 5EH
AL   = 03H
BX   = redirection list index
ES:DI = segment:offset of buffer to receive setup string

Returns:

If function successful
Carry flag = clear
CX   = length of printer setup string
ES:DI = address of buffer holding setup string

If function unsuccessful
Carry flag = set
AX   = error code

Notes:

■ The redirection list index passed in register BX is obtained with Function 5FH Subfunction 02H (Get Redirection List Entry).

■ See also Int 21H Function 5EH Subfunction 02H, which is used to specify a setup string for a network printer.

Int 21H Function 5FH (95)   [3.1]
Subfunction 02H
Get Redirection List Entry

Allows inspection of the system redirection list, which associates local logical names with network files, directories, or printers. This function call is only available when Microsoft Networks is running and the file-sharing module (SHARE.EXE) has been loaded.

Call with:

AH   = 5FH
AL   = 02H
BX   = redirection list index
DS:SI = segment:offset of 16-byte buffer to hold local device
          name
ES:DI = segment:offset of 128-byte buffer to hold network
          name

Returns:

If function successful
Carry flag = clear
BH   = device status flag
              bit 0   = 0 if device valid
                      = 1 if not valid
BL   = device type
              03H   if printer
              04H   if drive
CX   = stored parameter value
DX   = destroyed
BP   = destroyed
DS:SI   = segment:offset of ASCIIZ local device name
ES:DI   = segment:offset of ASCIIZ network name

If function unsuccessful
Carry flag = set
AX   = error code

Note:

- The parameter returned in CX is a value that was previously passed to MS-DOS in register CX with Int 21H Function 5FH Subfunction 03H (Redirect Device). It represents data that is private to the applications which store and retrieve it, and has no meaning to MS-DOS.

Int 21H Function 5FH (95)   [3.1]
Subfunction 03H
Redirect Device

Establishes redirection across the network by associating a local device name with a network name. This function call is only available when Microsoft Networks is running and the file-sharing module (SHARE.EXE) has been loaded.

Call with:

AH   = 5FH
AL   = 03H
BL   = device type
        03H   if printer
        04H   if drive

CX	= parameter to save for caller
DS:SI	= segment:offset of ASCIIZ local device name
ES:DI	= segment:offset of ASCIIZ network name, followed by ASCIIZ password

Returns:

If function successful
Carry flag = clear

If function unsuccessful
Carry flag = set
AX = error code

Notes:

■ The local name can be a drive designator (a letter followed by a colon, such as "D:"), a printer name, or a null string. Printer names must be one of the following: PRN, LPT1, LPT2, or LPT3. If a null string followed by a password is used, MS-DOS attempts to grant access to the network directory with the specified password.

■ The parameter passed in CX can be retrieved by later calls to Int 21H Function 5FH Subfunction 02H. It represents data that is private to the applications which store and retrieve it, and has no meaning to MS-DOS.

Int 21H Function 5FH (95) [3.1]
Subfunction 04H
Cancel Device Redirection

Cancels a previous redirection request by removing the association of a local device name with a network name. This function call is only available when Microsoft Networks is running and the file-sharing module (SHARE.EXE) has been loaded.

Call with:

AH	= 5FH
AL	= 04H
DS:SI	= segment:offset of ASCIIZ local device name

Returns:

If function successful
Carry flag = clear

If function unsuccessful
Carry flag = set
AX = error code

Note: .

- The supplied name can be a drive designator (a letter followed by a colon, such as "D:"), a printer name, or a string starting with two backslashes (\\). Printer names must be one of the following: PRN, LPT1, LPT2, or LPT3. If the string with two backslashes is used, the connection between the local machine and the network directory is terminated.

Int 21H Function 60H (96) [3]
Reserved

Int 21H Function 61H (97) [3]
Reserved

Int 21H Function 62H (98) [3]
Get PSP Address

Obtains the segment (paragraph) address of the program segment prefix (PSP) for the currently executing program.

Call with:

AH = 62H

Returns:

BX = segment address of program segment prefix

Notes:

- Before a program receives control from MS-DOS, its program segment prefix is set up to contain certain vital information, such as:
  - the segment address of the program's environment block;
  - the command line originally entered by the user;
  - the original contents of the terminate, Ctrl-C, and critical-error handler vectors;
  - and the top address of available RAM.

- The segment address of the PSP is normally passed to the program in registers DS and ES when it initially receives control from MS-DOS. This function allows a program to conveniently recover the PSP address at any point during its execution, without having to save it at program entry.

Int 21H Function 63H (99) [2.25 only]
Get Lead Byte Table

Obtains the address of the system table of legal lead byte ranges for extended character sets, or sets or obtains the interim console flag. Int 21H Function 63H is available only in MS-DOS version 2.25; it is not supported in MS-DOS version 3.

Call with:

AH	= 63H
AL	= subfunction

00H	*if getting address of system lead byte table*
01H	*if setting or clearing interim console flag*
02H	*if obtaining value of interim console flag*

If AL = 01H

DL	= 00H	if clearing interim console flag
	01H	if setting interim console flag

Returns:

If function successful
Carry flag = clear

and, if called with AL=00H
DS:SI = segment:offset of lead byte table

or, if called with AL=02H
DL = value of interim console flag

If function unsuccessful
Carry flag = set
AX = error code

Notes:

- The lead byte table consists of a variable number of 2-byte entries, terminated by 2 null (00H) bytes. Each pair defines the beginning and ending value for a range of lead bytes. The value of a legal lead byte is always in the range 80–0FFH.

- Entries in the lead byte table must be in ascending order. If no legal lead bytes are defined in a given system, the table consists only of the two null bytes.

- If the interim console flag is set, Int 21H Functions 07H (Unfiltered Character Input), 08H (Character Input without Echo), and 0BH (Keyboard Status) will support interim characters.

- Unlike most other MS-DOS services, this function call does not necessarily preserve any registers except SS:SP.

Int 21H Function 64H (100)   [3]
Reserved

Int 21H Function 65H (101)   [3.3]
Get Extended Country Information

Obtains information about the specified country and/or code page.

Call with:

AH	= 65H
AL	= subfunction
	01H = Get General Internationalization Information
	02H = Get Pointer to Uppercase Table
	04H = Get Pointer to Filename Uppercase Table
	06H = Get Pointer to Collating Table
BX	= code page of interest (-1 = active CON device)
CX	= length of buffer to receive information
DX	= country ID (-1 = default)
ES:DI	= address of buffer to receive information

Returns:

If function successful
Carry flag = clear

and requested data placed in calling program's buffer

If function unsuccessful
Carry flag = set
AX   = error code

Notes:

- The information returned by this function is a superset of the information returned by Int 21H Function 38H.

- This function may fail if either the country code or the code page number is invalid or if the code page does not match the country code.

- The function fails if the specified buffer length is less than five bytes. If the buffer to receive the information is at least five bytes long but is too short for the requested information, the data is truncated and no error is returned.

- The format of the data returned by Subfunction 01H is:

Byte(s)	Contents
00H	Information ID code (1)
01H–02H	Length of following buffer
03H–04H	Country ID
05H–06H	Code page number
07H–08H	Date format
	0 = USA m d y
	1 = Europe d m y
	2 = Japan y m d
09H–0DH	ASCIIZ currency symbol
0EH–0FH	ASCIIZ thousands separator
10H–11H	ASCIIZ decimal separator
12H–13H	ASCIIZ date separator
14H–15H	ASCIIZ time separator
16H	Currency format flags
	bit 0 = 0 if currency symbol precedes value
	* = 1 if currency symbol follows value*
	bit 1 = 0 if no space between value and currency symbol
	* = 1 if one space between value and currency symbol*

17H	Number of digits after decimal in currency
18H	Time format
	bit 0 = 0 if 12-hour clock
	= 1 if 24-hour clock
19H–1CH	Case-map routine call address
1DH–1EH	ASCIIZ data list separator
1FH–28H	Reserved

■ The format of the data returned by Subfunctions 02H, 04H, and 06H is:

Byte(s)	*Contents*
00H	Information ID code (2, 4, or 6)
01H–04H	Double-word pointer to table

■ The uppercase and filename uppercase tables are a maximum of 130 bytes long. The first two bytes contain the size of the table; the following bytes contain the uppercase equivalents, if any, for character codes 80H–FFH. The main use of these tables is to map accented or otherwise modified vowels to their plain vowel equivalents. Text translated with the help of this table can be sent to devices that do not support the IBM graphics character set, or used to create filenames that do not require a special keyboard configuration for entry.

■ The collating table is a maximum of 258 bytes long. The first two bytes contain the table length, and the subsequent bytes contain the values to be used for the corresponding character codes (0–FFH) during a sort operation. This table maps uppercase and lowercase ASCII characters to the same collating codes so that sorts will be case-insensitive, and it maps accented vowels to their plain vowel equivalents.

■ In some cases a truncated translation table may be presented to the program by MS-DOS. Applications should always check the length at the beginning of the table to ensure that it contains a translation code for the particular character of interest.

Int 21H Function 66H (102)   [3.3]
Get or Set Code Page

Obtains or selects the current code page.

Called with:

AH = 66H
AL = subfunction
  01H = Get Code Page
  02H = Select Code Page
BX = code page to select, if AL = 02H

Returns:

If function successful
Carry flag = clear

and, if called with AL = 01H
BX = active code page
DX = default code page

If function unsuccessful
Carry flag = set
AX = error code

Note:

■ When the Select Code Page subfunction is used, MS-DOS gets the new code page from the COUNTRY.SYS file. The device must be previously prepared for code page switching with the appropriate DEVICE= directive in the CONFIG.SYS file and NLSFUNC and MODE CP PREPARE commands (usually placed in the AUTOEXEC.BAT file).

Int 21H Function 67H (103) Set Handle Count   [3.3]

Sets the maximum number of files and devices that may be opened simultaneously using handles by the current process.

Call with:

AH = 67H
BX = number of desired handles

Returns:

If function successful
Carry flag = clear

If function unsuccessful
Carry flag = set
AX = error code

Notes:

■ This function call controls the size of the table that relates handle numbers for the current process to MS-DOS's internal, global table for all of the open files and devices in the system. The default table is located in the reserved area of the process's PSP and is large enough for 20 handles.

■ The function fails if the requested number of handles is greater than 20 and there is not sufficient free memory in the system to allocate a new block to hold the enlarged table.

■ If the number of handles requested is larger than the available entries in the system's global table for file and device handles (controlled by the FILES entry in CONFIG.SYS), no error is returned. However, a subsequent attempt to open a file or device, or create a new file, will fail if all of the entries in the system's global file table are in use, even if the requesting process has not used up all of its own handles.

Int 21H Function 68H (104)   [3.3]
Commit File

Forces all data in MS-DOS's internal buffers associated with a specified handle to be physically written to the device. If the handle refers to a file, and the file has been modified, the time and date stamp and file size in the file's directory entry are updated.

Call with:

AH   = 68H
BX   = handle

Returns:

If function successful
Carry flag = clear

If function unsuccessful
Carry flag = set
AX   = error code

Notes:

■ The effect of this function is equivalent to closing and reopening a file, or to duplicating a handle for the file with Int 21H Function 45H and then closing the duplicate. However, this function has the advantage that it will not fail due to lack of handles, and the application does not risk losing control of the file in multitasking or network environments.

■ If this function is requested for a handle associated with a character device, a success flag is returned but there is no other effect.

Int 22H [1] [2] [3]
Terminate Handler Address

The machine interrupt vector for Int 22H (memory locations 0000:0088H through 0000:008BH) contains the address of the routine that receives control when the currently executing program terminates via Int 20H, Int 27H, or Int 21H Functions 00H, 31H, or 4CH. The address in this vector is also copied into offsets 0AH through 0DH of the program segment prefix (PSP) when a program is loaded but before it begins executing, and is restored from the PSP (in case it was modified by the application) as part of MS-DOS's termination handling.

This interrupt should never be issued directly.

Int 23H [1] [2] [3]
Ctrl-C Handler Address

The machine interrupt vector for Int 23H (memory locations 0000:008CH though 0000:008FH) contains the address of the routine which receives control when a Ctrl-C is detected during any character I/O function and, if the Break flag is ON, during most other MS-DOS function calls. The address in this vector is also copied into locations 0EH through 11H of the program segment prefix (PSP) when a program is loaded but before it begins executing, and is restored from the PSP (in case it was modified by the application) as part of MS-DOS's termination handling.

This interrupt should never be issued directly.

Notes:

■ The initialization code for an application can use Int 21H Function 25H to reset the Interrupt 23H vector to point to its own routine for Ctrl-C handling. In this way, the program can avoid being terminated unexpectedly as the result of the user's entry of a Ctrl-C or Ctrl-Break.

- When a Ctrl-C is detected and the program's Int 23H handler receives control, all registers are set to their values at the point of the original function call. The handler can then do any of the following:
  - Set a local flag for later inspection by the application, or take any other appropriate action, and perform an IRET. All registers must be preserved. The MS-DOS function in progress will be restarted from scratch and will proceed to completion, control finally returning to the application in the normal manner.
  - Take appropriate action and then perform a RET FAR to give control back to MS-DOS. The state of the carry flag is used by MS-DOS to determine what action to take. If the carry flag is set, the application will be terminated; if the carry flag is clear, the application will continue in the normal manner.
  - Retain control by transferring to an error-handling routine within the application and then resume execution or take other appropriate action, never performing a RET FAR or IRET to end the interrupt-handling sequence. This option will cause no harm to the system.
- Any MS-DOS function call may be used within the body of an Int 23H handler.

Int 24H [1] [2] [3]
Critical-Error Handler Address

The machine interrupt vector for Int 24H (memory locations 0000:0090H through 0000:0093H) contains the address of the routine that receives control when a critical error (usually a hardware error) is detected. This address is also copied into locations 12H through 15H of the program segment prefix (PSP) when a program is loaded but before it begins executing, and is restored from the PSP (in case it was modified by the application) as part of MS-DOS's termination handling.

This interrupt should never be issued directly.

Notes:

- On entry to the critical-error interrupt handler, bit 7 of register AH is clear (0) if the error was a disk I/O error; otherwise, it is set (1). BP:SI contains the address of a device-driver header from which additional information can be obtained. Interrupts are disabled. The registers will be set up for a retry operation, and an error code will be in the lower half of the DI register, with the upper half undefined.

The lower byte of DI contains:

00H	write-protect error
01H	unknown unit
02H	drive not ready
03H	unknown command
04H	data error (CRC)
05H	bad request structure length
06H	seek error
07H	unknown media type
08H	sector not found
09H	printer out of paper
0AH	write fault
0BH	read fault
0CH	general failure
0DH	reserved
0EH	reserved
0FH	invalid disk change (MS-DOS 3.x only)

Note that these are the same error codes returned by the device driver in the request header. Also, upon entry, the stack is set up as follows:

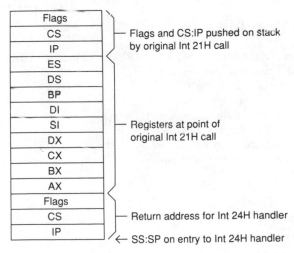

- When a disk I/O error occurs, MS-DOS automatically retries the operation before issuing a critical-error Int 24H. The number of retries varies in different versions of MS-DOS but is typically in the range three to five.

- Int 24H handlers must preserve the SS, SP, DS, ES, BX, CX, and DX registers. Only Int 21H Functions 01–0CH and 59H can be used by an Int 24H handler; other function calls will destroy the MS-DOS stack and its ability to retry or ignore an error.

- When the Int 24H handler issues an IRET, it should return an action code in AL that will be interpreted by DOS as follows:

  0   ignore the error
  1   retry the operation
  2   terminate the program
  3   [3] fail the function call in progress

- If the Int 24H handler returns control directly to the application program rather than to MS-DOS, it must restore the program's registers, removing all but the last three words from the stack, and issue an IRET. Control returns to the instruction immediately following the function call that caused the error. This option leaves MS-DOS in an unstable state until a call to an Int 21H function higher than Function 0CH is made.

Int 25H   [1] [2] [3]
Absolute Disk Read

Provides a direct linkage to the MS-DOS BIOS module to read data from a logical disk sector into memory.

Call with:

AL	= drive number (0=A, 1=B, etc)
CX	= number of sectors to read
DX	= starting sector number
DS:BX	= segment:offset of buffer

Returns:

If function successful
Carry flag = clear

If function unsuccessful
Carry flag = set
AX   = error code (see Notes)

Notes:

- All registers except the segment registers may be destroyed.

- When this function returns, the CPU flags originally pushed on the stack by the INT 25H instruction are *still* on the stack. The stack must be cleared by a POPF or ADD SP,2 to prevent uncontrolled stack growth, and to make accessible any other values that were pushed on the stack before the call to INT 25H.

- Logical sector numbers are obtained by numbering each disk sector sequentially from track 0, head 0, sector 1, and continuing until the last sector on the disk is counted. The head number is incremented before the track number. Logically adjacent sectors may not be physically adjacent, due to interleaving that occurs at the device-driver level for some disk types.

- The error code is interpreted as follows: The lower byte (AL) is the same error code that is returned in the lower byte of DI when an Int 24H is issued. The upper byte (AH) contains:

80H	if attachment failed to respond
40II	if seek operation failed
20H	if controller failed
10H	if data error (bad CRC)
08H	if direct memory access (DMA) failure
04H	if requested sector not found
02H	if bad address mark
01H	if bad command

Int 26H   [1] [2] [3]
Absolute Disk Write

Provides a direct linkage to the MS-DOS BIOS module to write data from memory to a logical disk sector.

Call with:

AL	= drive number (0=A, 1=B, etc)
CX	= number of sectors to write
DX	= starting sector number
DS:BX	= segment:offset of buffer

Returns:

If function successful
Carry flag = clear

If function unsuccessful
Carry flag = set
AX   = error code (see Notes)

Notes:

- All registers except the segment registers may be destroyed.

- When this function returns, the CPU flags originally pushed onto the stack by the INT 26H instruction are *still* on the stack. The stack must be cleared by a POPF or ADD SP,2 to prevent uncontrolled stack growth, and to make accessible any other values that were pushed on the stack before the call to INT 26H.

- Logical sector numbers are obtained by numbering each disk sector sequentially from track 0, head 0, sector 1, and continuing until the last sector on the disk is counted. The head number is incremented before the track number. Logically adjacent sectors may not be physically adjacent, due to interleaving that occurs at the device-driver level for some disk types.

- The error code is interpreted as follows: The lower byte (AL) is the same error code that is returned in the lower byte of DI when an Int 24H is issued. The upper byte (AH) contains:

80H	if attachment failed to respond
40H	if seek operation failed
20H	if controller failed
10H	if data error (bad CRC)
08H	if direct memory access (DMA) failure
04H	if requested sector not found
03H	if write-protect fault
02H	if bad address mark
01H	if bad command

Int 27H [1] [2] [3]
Terminate and Stay Resident

Terminates execution of the currently executing program, but reserves part or all of its memory so that it will not be overlaid by the next transient program to be loaded. MS-DOS then takes the following actions:

- File buffers are flushed and any open handles for files or devices owned by the process are closed.

- The termination handler vector (Int 22H) is restored from PSP:000AH.

- The Ctrl-C handler vector (Int 23H) is restored from PSP:000EH.
- [2] [3] The critical-error handler vector (Int 24H) is restored from PSP:0012H.
- Control is transferred to the termination handler.

If the program is returning to COMMAND.COM, control transfers to the resident portion and the transient portion is reloaded if necessary. If a batch file is in progress, the next line of the file is fetched and interpreted; otherwise a prompt is issued for the next user command.

Call with:

DX = offset of the last byte plus one (relative to the program segment prefix) of program to be protected

CS = segment of program segment prefix

Returns:

Nothing

Notes:

- This function call is typically used to allow user-written utilities, drivers, or interrupt handlers to be loaded as ordinary .COM or .EXE programs, and then remain resident. Subsequent entrance to the code is via a hardware or software interrupt.

- This function attempts to set the initial memory allocation block to the length *in bytes* specified in register DX. If other memory blocks have been requested by the application via Int 21H Function 48H, they will not be released by this function.

- Other methods of performing a final exit are:
  - Int 20H
  - Int 21H Function 00H
  - Int 21H Function 31H
  - Int 21H Function 4CH

- This function should not be called by .EXE programs that are loaded at the high end of the transient program area (i.e., linked with the /HIGH switch), because doing so reserves the memory that is normally used by the transient part of COMMAND.COM. If COMMAND.COM cannot be reloaded, the system will fail.

- This function does not work correctly when DX contains values in the range 0FFF1H–0FFFFH. In this case, MS-DOS discards the high bit of the value in DX, resulting in the reservation of 32 KB less memory than was requested by the program.

- [3] If the program is running on a network, it should remove all locks it has placed on file regions before terminating.
- [2] [3] Int 21H Function 31H should be used in preference to this function because it supports return codes, allows larger amounts of memory to be reserved, and does not require CS to contain the segment of the program segment prefix.

Int 28H [1] [2] [3]
Reserved

Int 29H [1] [2] [3]
Reserved

Int 2AH [1] [2] [3]
Reserved

Int 2BH [1] [2] [3]
Reserved

Int 2CH [1] [2] [3]
Reserved

Int 2DH [1] [2] [3]
Reserved

Int 2EH [1] [2] [3]
Reserved

Int 2FH
Multiplex Interrupt

[3]

Provides a general-purpose avenue of communication with various
MS-DOS extensions, such as the print spooler and APPEND. These
extensions are typically loaded as terminate-and-stay-resident (TSR)
programs.

Int 2FH Function 01H
Print Spooler

[3]

Submits a file to the print spooler, removes a file from the print
spooler's queue of pending files, or obtains the status of the printer.
The print spooler, which is contained in the file PRINT.COM, was
first added to MS-DOS in version 2.0, but the application program in-
terface to the spooler was not documented until MS-DOS version 3.

Call with:

AH	= 01H
AL	= subfunction
	00H = Get Installed State
	01H = Submit File to be Printed
	02H = Remove File from Print Queue
	03H = Cancel All Files in Queue
	04H = Hold Print Jobs for Status Read
	05H = Release Hold
DS:DX	= segment:offset of packet (Subfunction 01H)
	segment:offset of ASCIIZ pathname (Subfunction 02H)

Returns:

If function successful
Carry flag = clear

and, if called with AL = 00H

AL	= print spooler state
	00H *if not installed, ok to install*
	01H *if not installed, not ok to install*
	FFH *if installed*

or, if called with AL = 04H

DX   = error count
DS:SI   = segment:offset of print queue file list

If function unsuccessful

Carry flag   = set
AX   = error code

Notes:

- The packet passed to Subfunction 01H consists of five bytes. The first byte contains the *level*, which should be 00H for MS-DOS versions 2 and 3. The following four bytes contain the segment:offset of an ASCIIZ pathname, which may not include wildcard characters. If the specified file exists, it is added to the print queue.

- The * and ? wildcard characters may be included in a pathname passed to Subfunction 02H, making it possible to delete multiple files from the print queue with one call.

- The address returned by Subfunction 04H points to a list of 64-byte entries, each containing an ASCIIZ pathname. The first pathname in the list is the file currently being printed. The last entry in the list is a null string (a single 00H byte).

The manuscript for this book was prepared and submitted to Microsoft Press in electronic form. Text files were processed and formatted using Microsoft Word.

Cover design by Ted Mader & Associates
Interior text design by Greg Hickman
Principal typography by Carol Luke

Text composition by Microsoft Press in Times Roman with display in Times Roman Bold, using the Magna composition system and the Linotronic 300 laser imagesetter.

OTHER TITLES FROM MICROSOFT PRESS

RUNNING MS-DOS®, 3rd edition
The Classic, Definitive Work on DOS—Now Completely Revised
and Expanded to Include All Versions of PC/MS-DOS®—Including
Hard-Disk Management Tips and Techniques

Van Wolverton

"This book is simply the definitive handbook of PC/MS-DOS...written
for both novices and experienced users." **BYTE**

Van Wolverton will guide you through hands-on examples of PC-DOS
and MS-DOS commands and capabilities. He will also show you how
to work with files and directories on a floppy- or hard-disk system;
how to effectively manage printers, monitors, and modems; how to
automate frequently performed tasks with batch files; and much more.
An expanded MS-DOS command reference is included. Covers
MS-DOS through version 3.3. RUNNING MS-DOS—accept no
substitutes.

512 pages, 7⅜ x 9¼, softcover $22.95 Order #86-96262
hardcover $35.00 Order #86-96270

SUPERCHARGING MS-DOS®
The Microsoft® Guide to High Performance Computing for the
Experienced PC User

Van Wolverton

"SUPERCHARGING MS-DOS is a valuable addition to any PC user's
reference library. For advanced MS-DOS users and software program-
mers it's a must." **Microtimes**

When you're ready for more power, this sequel to RUNNING
MS-DOS provides intermediate- to advanced-level tips on maximiz-
ing the power of MS-DOS. Control your screen and keyboard with
ANSI.SYS; create, examine, or change any file; and personalize your
CONFIG.SYS file. Includes programs and dozens of valuable batch
files.

320 pages, 7⅜ x 9¼, softcover $18.95 Order #86-95595

SUPERCHARGING MS-DOS is also available with a handy 5.25-
inch companion disk that contains scores of batch files, script files,
and programs from the book. Used in conjunction with the book, the
companion disk is a timesaving tool.

SUPERCHARGING MS-DOS Book/Disk Package

Van Wolverton

320 pages, softcover with one 5.25-inch disk $34.95
Order #86-96304

MICROSOFT® QUICKC™ PROGRAMMING
The Microsoft® Guide to Using the QuickC Compiler

The Waite Group: Mitchell Waite, Stephen Prata, Bryan Costales, and Harry Henderson

The most authoritative introduction to every significant element of Microsoft QuickC available today! The scores of programming examples and tips show you how to manipulate QuickC's variable types; how to program using the Graphics Library; how to port Pascal to QuickC; how to use the powerful source-level debugger; and more. If you're new to C, familiar with Microsoft QuickBASIC or Pascal, or a seasoned programmer, you'll find solid, advanced information that's available nowhere else.

608 pages, 7⅜ x 9¼, softcover $19.95 Order #86-96114

POWER WINDOWS
Maximizing the Speed and Performance of Windows 2.0 and Windows/386

Jim Heid

POWER WINDOWS is the only book with detailed information on Windows 2.0 and Windows/386. Heid shows you how to streamline your start-up procedures; create optimal configurations; customize the WIN.INI file; allocate memory for running applications; and much more. A special section describes the differences between Windows' versions.

304 pages, 7⅜ x 9¼, softcover $19.95 Order #86-96064

INSIDE OS/2

Gordon Letwin, Chief Architect, Systems Software, Microsoft
Foreword by Bill Gates

"Run, do not walk, to your nearest bookseller and buy a copy of the new Microsoft Press book INSIDE OS/2 by Gordon Letwin.... He knows OS/2. He can also write. It's not easy to produce a readable book about anything intrinsically dull as an operating system, but Letwin has done a surprisingly good job." **Infoworld**

INSIDE OS/2 is an unprecedented, candid, and exciting technical examination of OS/2. Letwin takes you inside the philosophy, key development issues, programming implications, and future of OS/2. A valuable and revealing programmer-to-programmer discussion. You can't get a more inside view. This is a book no OS/2 programmer can afford to be without!

304 pages, 7⅜ x 9¼, softcover $19.95 Order #86-96288